Understanding the Reading Needs of English Language Learners

Jeff Popko

ESOL for Different Professions Series

tesol
press

Typeset by Capitol Communications, LLC, Crofton, Maryland USA
and printed by Gasch Printing, LLC, Odenton, Maryland USA

TESOL Press
TESOL International Association
1925 Ballenger Avenue
Alexandria, Virginia 22314 USA
Tel 703-836-0774 • Fax 703-836-7864
www.tesol.org

Senior Manager, Publications: Myrna Jacobs
Cover Design: Tomiko Breland
Copy Editor: Tomiko Breland
Project Reviewer: Guofang Li

TESOL Book Publications Committee
    John Liontas, Chair
    Robyn Brinks-Lockwood, Co-Chair
    Margo DelliCarpini
    Deoksoon Kim
    Ilka Kostka
    Guofang Li
    Gilda Martinez-Alba
    Adrian J. Wurr

ISBN 9781942223559
Library of Congress Control Number 2014956005

Contents

Introduction

The teacher should clearly see whether the end to which a school exercise
looks is skill or knowledge-practical power or intellectual power.

Hinsdale (1896, p. 11)

nglish language learners (ELLs) come into the K–12 setting without the
strong preparation in English reading skills that native-English-speaking
(NES) students have had (Barone & Xu, 2008; Genesee, Lindholm-Leary,
Saunders, & Christian, 2006; Sousa, 2008; Syrja, 2011). Yet with 1 year of
English as a second language (ESL) classes, ELLs are expected to make up for
years of reading lessons and practice, and to read textbooks in English "at grade
level." English is the medium of instruction in the United States, so all students,
including ELLs, are expected to learn content material in all of their courses
(math, science, history) not just in their ESL or English language arts classes.
Because reading is the foundation for learning in every class, in many ways all
teachers are in part English teachers. Unfortunately, K–12 content-area teachers,
librarians, reading specialists, and support staff may not be trained to meet the
literacy needs of ELLs, even if they recognize those needs.

The underlying difference between ELLs' reading abilities and those of their
English-language-speaking peers is time and experience: In U.S. K–12 schools,
students learn how to read up to third grade. From fourth grade on, they are
expected to be able to read in order to learn. ELLs come into the U.S. school
system from a variety of language backgrounds and learning experiences and
are trying to learn how to read English while being expected to learn from the
readings that are assigned by teachers in their content-area classes. ELLs do not
learn to read at the same rate as their NES peers. Nor do all ELLs learn at the
same rate (Klingner, Almanza, de Onis, & Barletta, 2008; Orosco, de Schonewise,
de Onis, Klingner, & Hoover, 2008). Even within NES student populations, there

are clear differences in rate and level of achievement between students who have been exposed to large amounts of text and those who have not (Stanovich, 2000; Stanovich & Cunningham, 1993; Stanovich, & West, 1989; Stanovich, West, & Harrison, 1995).

In the field of teaching English to speakers of other languages, research has demonstrated that whereas ELLs can achieve basic interpersonal communicative skills in English within 2 years of living in an ESL community (Cummins, 1979, 2000, 2005), it takes an additional 5–7 years for the same students to catch up to their NES peers in the area of cognitive academic language proficiency. In other words, ELLs may be conversant in English, but they lack the language ability needed to learn age-appropriate content materials in the medium of English.

The reason for this lag is that ELLs are continuously playing catch-up with their NES peers, or as Pilgreen (2010) put it, "older students have more to achieve and less time to do it" (p. 2). NES students have a basic English vocabulary of about 5,000 words once they begin school (Stahl, 1999), although their "mastery of vocabulary acquisition . . . is still vastly incomplete" (Pythian-Sence & Wagner, 2007, p. 1). However, even ELLs who appear to be fluent in layman's terms—those who can carry out conversations about familiar topics in and around school settings—often have a vocabulary of only 2,000 of the most common words in English. This suggests that ELLs who can speak and understand basic conversational English when they enter U.S. schools still need to learn 3,000 new words in order to catch up to first-grade NES students. Each year, U.S. students expand their vocabularies through class work and extensive reading, raising the bar for English learning vocabulary targets, and widening the gap. Similar to the Matthew Effect, a theory that says that as faster readers read more, they get better at reading (Stanovich, 1986, 2000), NES students who have a higher entering vocabulary can be expected to expand their vocabulary knowledge faster than ELLs who have a lower entering vocabulary (Nation, 1990).

Given that ELLs are not reading at grade level, many face a downward spiral (Stahl, 1999; Stanovich, 2000): Because they have difficulty reading, they don't like to read; because they don't like to read, they don't read as much as their NES peers; because they don't read as much, their reading does not improve as quickly; because their reading does not improve, they get discouraged and don't like to read. The spiral starts over again (Cunningham & Stanovich, 1997).

Language is the medium of instruction in the United States, and the main source for new learning is reading. Textbooks are the primary source for all school content, but Cunningham and Stanovich (1997) found in their longitudinal study of K–12 students that those who read more outside the classroom surpassed their peers in every test category (including non-English subjects such as math and history) by a wide margin. When students cannot easily read at grade level, they find all of their lessons more difficult, and they are less likely to read for pleasure outside of class. Without appropriate reading skills, ELLs fall behind in history, science, math, and basic cultural capital. The purpose of this book is to explain the reading challenges ELLs face, and to present some suggestions for overcoming this basic limitation to their academic advancement.

Standards-Based Instruction 2

The U.S. educational system has for the last decade focused on standards-based teaching and assessment. Under the No Child Left Behind Act (2002) every state was required to create a set of standards in the core content areas. Most of these standards were based on work done by the various professional educational organizations. In 1997, Teachers of English to Speakers of Other Languages, Inc. (TESOL) published *ESL Standards for PreK–12 Students*, which became the basis for many state ESL standards. The TESOL standards were updated to *PreK–12 English Language Proficiency Standards* in 2006. These new standards have been used to inform the national debate by organizations such as the Council of Chief State School Officers & National Governors Association and the World Class Instructional Design and Assessment (WIDA) consortium.

Common Core Standards and English Language Learners

The National Governor's Association (NGA) and the Council of Chief State School Officers (CCSSO) have published the Common Core State Standards Initiative (NGA & CCSSO, 2010a) online. These standards, frequently referred to as the Common Core, have been adopted by 44 states in an effort to develop a consistent target for educational outcomes across the United States. One point on which the Common Core differ from previous curricula is the strong emphasis on English language across the curriculum. In the past, many schools have relegated the teaching of language to the English language arts (ELA) or ESL courses. The Common Core clearly focus on the teaching of language in every school subject. The standards for ELA are not relegated to one genre or subject, but are titled *Common Core State Standards for English Language Arts & Literacy in History/Social Studies, Science, and Technical Subjects:*

> The Standards insist that instruction in reading, writing, speaking, listening, and language be a shared responsibility within the school . . . expectations for reading, writing, speaking, listening, and language [are] applicable to a range of subjects, including but not limited to ELA . . . teachers in other areas must have a role in this development as well. (NGA & CCSSO, 2010b, p. 4)

The Common Core address the needs of English language learners (ELLs) in the publication *Application of Common Core State Standards for English Language Learners* (NGA & CCSSO, 2010d). Every teacher and administrator in the United States should read this three-page statement, whether they use the Common Core or a different set of standards. The statement notes:

> [ELLs] require additional time, appropriate instructional support, and aligned assessments as they acquire both English language proficiency and content area knowledge. . . . Effectively educating these students requires diagnosing each student instructionally, adjusting instruction accordingly, and closely monitoring student progress. (NGA & CCSSO, 2010d, p. 1)

The paper clearly states that ELLs' reading needs differ from NES students in attempting to meet the Common Core. The goal of educating ELLs, according to this paper, is to make them college-ready through meeting the same rigorous content standards as NES students in the United States. In order to reach this goal, the paper calls for:

- Highly qualified teachers who are certified in ESL instruction

- A school environment rich in literacy

- Language instruction to build foundational skills in English

- Comprehensible input: course work written in English the ELLs can understand

- Pair and group work that allows ELLs to use oral English to communicate

- Ongoing assessment

- Models of academic English

- Opportunities to code-switch between the ELLs' first language and English to accomplish complex tasks

- Language support to help students understand the English in story problems before being asked to solve them

- Opportunities for students to use English to discuss complex concepts (academic discourse)

Recognizing that "the development of native like proficiency in English takes many years and will not be achieved by all ELLs especially if they start schooling in the US in the later grades" (NGA & CCSSO, 2010d, p. 1), the authors nevertheless encourage schools to strive toward the Common Core through appropriate support by teachers who are highly qualified in ESL. Students can meet the standard in math whatever their home language, even though their accent, grammar, and vocabulary may never reach "native-speaker" proficiency. Therefore, the goal is not to have all ELLs speak English like NES students, but to provide them with at least the minimum language ability to engage academically at grade level in the core subject areas.

The Council for the Accreditation of Educator Preparation and ELLs

The National Council for the Accreditation of Teacher Education (NCATE) recently merged with the Teacher Education Accreditation Council (TEAC) to form the Council for the Accreditation of Educator Preparation (CAEP). The new agency works with numerous other professional organizations to assess teacher preparation programs. Where ELLs are involved, CAEP coordinated with TESOL International Association to develop the guidelines in the *TESOL P–12 ESL Professional Teaching Standards* (TESOL, 2010). These 13 standards are divided into 5 domains: Language, Culture, Instruction, Assessment, and Professionalism (Appendix A). Compared with the most recent National Council of Teachers of English *Standards for Initial Preparation of Teachers of Secondary English Language Arts, Grades 7–12* (NCTE, 2012), which have 23 elements for 7 standards divided into 5 domains.

Where the TESOL standards (2010) focus on language (including linguistics, grammar, and vocabulary), the NCTE standards (2012a) focus on literacy (literature and composition). Content knowledge in TESOL includes the ability to "use the major theories and research related to the structure and acquisition of language to help English language learners (ELLs) develop language and literacy" (p. 26), whereas NCTE focuses on reading "a range of different texts—across genres, periods, forms, authors, cultures, and various forms of media" and on "composing texts (i.e., oral, written, and visual)" (p. 1). For NCTE the structure of language is part of one element (element 5), namely, that good English teaching "incorporates knowledge of language—structure, history, and conventions" (p. 1), whereas for TESOL, knowledge of language is central. In Domain 1: Standard 1.a "Candidates demonstrate understanding of language as a system, including phonology, morphology, syntax, pragmatics and semantics, and support ELLs as they acquire English language and literacy in order to achieve in the content areas" (p. 27).

Another difference in the focus of the TESOL standards (for teachers of ELLs) and the NCTE standards (for teachers of NES students) is the weight of the focus on culture. For ELLs, TESOL requires that highly qualified teachers "know, understand, and use the major concepts, principles, theories, and research related to the nature and role of culture and cultural groups to construct learning environments that support ESOL students' cultural identities, language and literacy development, and content-area achievement" (p. 38). NCTE, on the other hand, includes ELLs within societal diversity, as teachers are required to plan and teach lessons that are "accessible to all students, including English language learners, students with special needs, students from diverse language and learning backgrounds, those designated as high achieving, and those at risk of failure" (p. 1).

> **Take Away** ELLs form part of the audience for ELA teaching. CAEP distinguishes between highly qualified ELA teachers and highly qualified teachers of ELLs. Teaching English to those who already know the language is a different skill and requires different methods than teaching students for whom English is an additional (perhaps second, third, or fourth) language. To be considered "highly qualified" to work with ELLs, a teacher must be trained in the specialized field of TESOL.

Sheltered English Instruction

One of the most popular programs for teaching ELLs in the United States is the sheltered English instruction (SEI) model.[1] In SEI, ELLs are placed in content classrooms together, so that the teacher (e.g., in math or science) can work together with an ESL teacher to create lesson plans that meet the school's standards in the content area while providing the ELLs with scaffolded support to learn English. In other words, ELLs study the same content as NES students, while their English study stems from the academic content. SEI allows content and ESL teachers to collaborate, applying their knowledge together so that ELLs learn English without falling behind in the other content areas.

The Center for Applied Linguistics provides materials and training in SEI, including materials for perhaps the most widely used SEI model, the Sheltered Instruction Observation Protocol (SIOP; Echevarria, Vogt, & Short, 2004). SIOP is a programmatic system of improving ELL learning outcomes. In typical SIOP models, the content teacher collaborates with the TESOL teacher in eight key areas: preparation, building background, comprehensible input, strategies, interaction, practice/application, lesson delivery, and review/assessment. Teacher pairs work to improve each of these areas of teaching in order. To monitor progress, teachers are observed using the checklist protocol (Appendix B). While the SIOP model is comprehensive in nature, dealing with all four skills and every content area, it highlights many key aspects of differentiation between NES students' and ELLs' reading. The most important underlying theme is that for ELLs, reading instruction must be integrated across the curriculum, not delegated solely to the ELA classroom.

[1] This should not be confused with the Arizona Structured English Immersion (SEI) program of isolated English instruction that prevents ELLs from learning content material until after they have reached a target English test score.

The Center for Applied Linguistics text *What's Different About Teaching Reading to Students Learning English? Study Guide* (Kaufman, 2007) and related professional workshops are highly recommended for TESOL professionals who would like more in-depth information that is beyond the scope of this book.

Take Away Decades of research have produced clear indications that reading instruction is vital to ELL success in schools. The most promising methods for ELL success in school do not teach reading apart, but integrate the teaching of reading across the curriculum, through the school year, and throughout grades P–12.

Language Needs of ELLs

3

Consider the following questions:
- *What do students need to know in order to read at grade level?*
- *What advantages do NES students have over English language learners (ELLs) in learning to read?*

Students use both linguistic and cultural knowledge in order to comprehend texts. As a result, native English speakers who have been surrounded with a culture of literacy in the United States have an advantage over ELLs (and over NES students in the United States who did not grow up surrounded by academic literacy). First, ELLs need to improve their English language skills (vocabulary and grammar) to catch up to native English speakers. Oral language ability is a prerequisite to literacy (Genesee et al., 2006). Second, ELLs need to build their historical and cultural background knowledge to comprehend such conventions as literary allusion and metaphor found throughout academic reading material. In fact, the NGA & CCSSI (2010b) encourage use of "reading great classic and contemporary works of literature representative of a variety of periods, cultures, and worldviews" (p. 7) for all students, but choosing culturally appropriate reading materials is particularly important for ELLs. Third, ELLs need to learn the range of genres required for academic success in the United States. Finally, ELLs need to learn to navigate the academic literacy culture of the U.S. education system (Sousa, 2011).

It can be tempting to keep the discussion of native English speakers and ELLs focused on a simple dichotomy. However, any classroom teacher knows that NES students represent a continuum of reading ability levels: No Child Left Behind (NCLB; 2002) requires that all students take tests of reading ability.

Nationwide, these reading tests show a wide division between the highest- and lowest-achieving NES students' scores according to the National Reading Panel's 2000 report (National Reading Panel, 2000). Likewise, ELLs fall into a wide continuum, based on their home language, age upon arrival in the United States, number of years of education, and time spent in dedicated ESL or bilingual classrooms. Rather than focus on the upper end of the English ability scale for ELLs (functionally bilingual children), this book is focused on those students most in need of support: new arrivals and those who have received little or no English language support. In other words, this book is intended to shed light on the needs of ELLs requiring language support.

Given this focus, there are five specific areas of language that require special attention if ELLs are to catch up to their NES peers' academic reading level: Vocabulary, grammar, language learning strategies, reading fluency, and background knowledge (both sociocultural and linguistic).

Vocabulary

Consider the following questions:
- *How many words do you know?*
- *How many words does the average student know at each level, K–12?*
- *How many words do ELLs entering at each level (K–12) know?*
- *What does it mean to know vocabulary? [aural recognition, pronunciation, reading recognition, spelling, appropriate use in writing, appropriate use in speaking, forms such as tense/plural, families, denotations, connotations, metaphoric use]*
- *What are the right words to know/teach?*

As mentioned in the introduction, ELLs will be well behind NES students in the area of vocabulary development, no matter when they began schooling. Naturally, when ELLs begin U.S. schooling at higher levels, they have correspondingly large gaps in needed vocabulary. Research indicates that for a student to read comfortably for pleasure, he or she needs to know 95% of the words in a given text (Carver, 1994; Laufer, 1989). Recent studies in reading fluency suggest that students can learn from texts if they know at least 95% of the vocabulary of the text, but that they are not comfortable reading if they know fewer than 98% of the words in a given text, particularly in academic texts (Nagy, 2005).

A good review of the current research on vocabulary acquisition and teaching can be found in Pressley, Disney, and Anderson (2007). They point out eight keys to teaching vocabulary that are recommended for all students:

1. Provide a rich vocabulary environment

2. Require extensive reading

3. Pay attention to students and help them when they are struggling to understand a word

4. Provide definitions, especially with appropriate dictionaries

5. Expose students to words numerous times in print and orally

6. Teach students to use context to learn meanings of new words

7. Teach students the meanings of common affixes

8. Require students to interact with target words analytically (pp. 223–224)

ELLs can learn vocabulary in much the same way, but teachers should always keep in mind that ELLs form a diverse range of backgrounds. Some ELLs will have cognates for English words in their own languages (for example, Spanish speakers can easily recognize the connection between *especial* and *special*), and others will not. Also, a shared writing system, as used in European languages, will simplify the vocabulary learning process. According to the Common Core documents:

> ELLs who are literate in a first language that shares cognates with English can apply first-language vocabulary knowledge when reading in English; likewise ELLs with high levels of schooling can often bring to bear conceptual knowledge developed in their first language when reading in English. However, ELLs with limited or interrupted schooling will need to acquire background knowledge prerequisite to educational tasks at hand. (NGA & CCSSO, 2010d, p. 1)

U.S. students learn approximately 3,000 new words per year (Stahl, 1999), reaching an estimated 38,000 words known by the time they reach university. Of course, many of these words are synonyms, and others are low-frequency words that are not crucial to reading comprehension. ELLs, on the other hand, may begin with zero English vocabulary words, and learn closer to 1,000 words per year on average, reaching fewer than 12,000 words known after 12th grade (Figure 1). It is highly likely that an ELL will never catch up to her or his NES peers, given the massive head start of the latter. Fortunately, as noted above, "catching up" is not the goal: Successful academic learning is the goal. Estimates of the vocabulary needed for ELLs to succeed in university start at as low as 9,000 words (Schmitt, Jiang, & Grabe, 2011; Schmitt & Schmitt, 2013; Laufer & Nation, 1995; Nation, 1993). That still leaves 7,000 words for ELLs to learn after they have reached a comfortable level of basic interpersonal communicative skills if they are going to be "college-ready" (NGA & CCSSO, 2010d).

In order to bridge this gap, a coherent school-wide approach is needed. Rather than expecting ELLs to catch up through ESL pullout classes, English language arts (ELA), or unstructured inclusion, "students, teachers, materials writers, and researchers . . . need to acknowledge the incremental nature of vocabulary learning, and to develop learning programs which are principled, long-term, and which recognize the richness and cope of the lexical knowledge that needs to be mastered" (Schmitt, 2008, p. 329).

It is true that vocabulary is unique to each individual. Where one grows up, for example, may determine whether or not one knows the difference between a *picket fence* and a *picket pen*. Words and sayings used by one's parents and

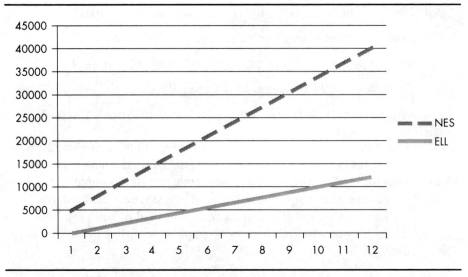

Figure 1. Estimated Vocabulary Knowledge of NES and ELL Students at Each Grade Level

grandparents will often differ even between families in the same town. But there are lists of core vocabulary that ELLs need. This includes both core vocabulary for daily communication and the core academic vocabulary of the school setting. Once students specialize in a particular content area (e.g., majoring in economics) they will also need to learn the core vocabulary of their chosen field (not every student needs to know *actuarial* or *cataphoric*).

There are a variety of lists that a school might use specifically for ELLs. Nation (1991) suggested a basic communication list of 2,000 headwords with 8,000 additional academic words to prepare students for university. Schmitt and Schmitt (2013) suggest increasing the list to 3,000 high-frequency words that should provide ELLs with an adequate basis for learning, e.g., the Oxford 3000 list. He suggests a larger list of an additional 6,000 targeted words to prepare for university. Coxhead's academic word list (AWL; Coxhead, 2000) provides the 570 headwords that most commonly appear in academic texts across school subject areas. Gardner and Davies (2014) provide a list of 3,000 academic words that are not presented as headwords. Neufeld and Billuroğlu (2006) combined lists of frequent and academic vocabulary to create a six-level list (called the BNL) of vocabulary (plus a *zero level* of function words) of 2,709 headwords that include 90–95% of vocabulary found in academic texts.

The key is to pick a list of high-frequency and key academic words that fit your curriculum and incorporate it systematically in teaching. The BNL list is perhaps the most flexible. It is recent and represents the foundational vocabulary that ELLs should recognize in order to comprehend academic texts in order to succeed in U.S. universities.

Most textbooks provide some vocabulary development by marking the target words for a chapter in bold and/or including a definition for the word in a glossary at the back of the book. Words that are taught by textbook authors are those that U.S. NES students need to learn to master the material. ELLs need more. The textbook might list *sum* as a vocabulary word to learn, but ELL students also need to know that *add*, *plus*, and *and* mean the same thing: 2 *added* to 2; 2 *plus* 2; 2 *and* 2. Moreover, ELLs need to understand the prepositions associated with math: 2 *by* 2; 2 *into* 2; 2 *of* 2; 2 *for* 2. If they are taught only the glossary terms, ELLs will not be able to learn the language necessary to read and understand the book.

There is, then, a difference between the vocabulary that ELLs need and the vocabulary typically taught in K–12 classes. Consider the three tiers of vocabulary (Beck & McKeown, 1985; Beck, McKeown, & Omanson, 1987) acknowledged by the Common Core (NGGA & CCSSO, 2010a). NES students come to school having developed a sense of vocabulary from their oral language maturation, and perhaps from having been read to in English and even having learned to read simple texts. Their English vocabulary, including words needed for daily communication, begins forming in child/parent interactions (e.g., *mommy, daddy, go, come, like, eat*). These are *Tier 1* words. They represent the most common 2,000–3,000 words on the word lists. ELLs have developed this core vocabulary not in English, but in their home language.

NES children then expand their vocabularies to include the function words of English (e.g., prepositions, articles, adverbs of time and place). These are part of the *Tier 2* vocabulary words covered in the BNL level 0. They are needed to understand more difficult texts and interactions as texts move away from language of here and now to language used to discuss actions by other people elsewhere. When NES children arrive in school, they have a strong foundation of Tier 1 and 2 vocabulary, and they are ready to learn the *Tier 3* words: those needed to engage academically in class (e.g., words needed to study math, science, and social studies). These include the words on academic lists like the AWL and the Academic Vocabulary List (AVL), and subject-specific words (e.g., *quadrilateral, rhizome*). Typically, K–12 teachers focus on expanding Tier 3 vocabulary of the subject-specific words. The assumption is that the majority of students already have a strong foundation of Tier 1 and Tier 2 words. Students are expected to learn the Tier 1, Tier 2, and function words in Tier 3 (e.g., *inclusive, analysis*) as they read. NES students can do this because they are fluent enough readers that they can connect new word meanings to their available vocabulary knowledge.

ELLs do not have a large base vocabulary. They will find it difficult to pick up new Tier 1 and Tier 2 words. They are unlikely to learn Tier 3 words without direct instruction. For example, an ELL may have only one word for a piece of furniture to sit on: *chair*. NES students, on the other hand, know from their home language development that one may sit on a *chair, couch, stool*, or *bench*. While it makes sense when teaching NES students, the ELL may not benefit from the statement "*Sofa* is another word for *couch*." ELLs who have not been explicitly taught the vocabulary might find it difficult to distinguish between a test item that asks them to *summarize* a text and one that asks them to *analyze* it.

Having been provided with a principled list of target words in a school-wide system of vocabulary development, students can begin to take control of their own vocabulary learning process. However, it is also important to emphasize the incremental nature of vocabulary learning (Nagy & Scott, 2014). Each word must be presented, recycled, reviewed, and used in a variety of ways over time. According to Nagy and Scott (2014), "when students are dependent on instruction to learn a word . . . that instruction must provide multiple and varied encounters with that word" (p. 273).

Take Away ELLs do not need to learn all the vocabulary known by NES students to succeed in school. They do, however, need to learn thousands of words of vocabulary that NES students already know. For this reason, ELLs require explicit instruction in vocabulary even at the most basic level in order to catch up to their NES peers. Rather than studying only Tier 3 words (found in most textbook glossaries), ELLs need to study and be taught Tier 1 and Tier 2 vocabulary.

Grammar

Consider the following questions:
- What makes a high school textbook more difficult to read than a fourth-grade textbook?
- What are the parts of speech in English? Do you think they are the same in other languages? What part of speech is to eat? To live? Think about: To eat is to live.
- What parts of speech should ELLs focus on if they would like to comprehend the gist of a reading text? Notwithstanding the diners' clear preference for beef, the cooks at the small cafeteria served bland and overcooked chicken time after time.
- How might variations in English grammar cause misunderstandings while reading?

Children who grow up surrounded by and using English have a strong head start when beginning to read. By the time students reach school age, they have internalized the majority of grammatical structures needed to function within the society (Genesee et al., 2006). Children naturally learn the underlying linguistic systems of their languages: phonology (i.e., pronunciation), morphology (e.g., plurals and tense markers), syntax (e.g., word order; English is a "subject–verb–object" language while Japanese is "subject–object–verb" language), semantics (i.e., vocabulary), and pragmatics (i.e., appropriate use of language in context, such as politeness markers). Native-speaker intuition of the language tells U.S. NES students that there are different parts of speech (e.g., nouns are different from verbs). It helps them to recognize patterns in the language (e.g., –ed, whether pronounced /t/, /d/, or /–Ud/, marks the regular past tense). By listening and speaking alone, they have automatized (Samuels, 2004) the use of articles and prepositions, word order, and a host of collocations (e.g., English speakers say *black and white* where Spanish speakers always say *blanco y negro*—white and black) along with many other grammatical items. Before they begin to read, U.S. NES students know intuitively how to correctly use masculine versus feminine pronouns, that adjectives come before nouns, the forms of irregular verbs such as *be* and *eat*, and more. ELLs, whose first language intuition is very different, must learn these language structures.

Linguists generally believe that age and maturation play a key role in language learning. The critical age hypothesis states that people who begin learning a second language after the age of puberty (as many ELLs do) will never gain native speaker proficiency with their second language. Not only phonology/pronunciation, but also such grammatical constructs as pronouns, articles, and markers of masculine/feminine tend to cause ELLs difficulty their entire lives.

As with vocabulary, grammar is an area where ELLs are playing catch-up. Each year of school presents U.S. NES students with new grammatical complexity. Knowing the basics of the language such as parts of speech, they gradually learn that phrases and then clauses can act together as nouns, verbs, adjectives, adverbs, and prepositions. They begin to learn principles of deletion—that not every word needs to appear in the text. For example, passive voice assumes the final prepositional phrase, which can therefore be removed: The cake was eaten *by the boy*. NES students learn year by year not to be confused when words have been removed for stylistic reasons. ELLs who are attempting to read at the same age level as their NES peers have not had the same long-term engagement with these often untaught rules of English.

The Common Core *College and Career Readiness Anchor Standards for Language* specifically state that all students should "demonstrate command of the conventions of standard English grammar and usage when writing or speaking" (NGA & CCSSO, 2010b, p. 51). They do not directly address grammar or linguistic knowledge for ELLs. However, the *Application for English Learners* (NGA & CCSSO, 2010d) does note that schools need to adopt and meet "language proficiency standards that teachers can use in conjunction with the ELA standards to assist ELLs in becoming proficient and literate in English" (p. 1). The most widely used standards for ESL are the *PreK–12 English Language Proficiency Standards* (TESOL, 2006).

To read proficiently, more is required than learning grammatical rules and various exceptions to those rules. Concepts that underlie the rules create nuances of meaning within the text. It is necessary to internalize how grammar works in context, within discourse rather than at the sentence level alone (Larsen-Freeman, 2001, 2003). NES students who read extensively outside of the classroom have been shown to perform far above their classmates who do not (Cunningham & Stanovich, 1997), but even those NES students who read only what is assigned by their teachers have read thousands of pages of English per year more than the ELL who enters the U.S. school system in middle school. Imagine the disadvantage of a novice tennis player who enters a class with peers who have practiced 6 hours a day for several years. ELLs lack the time on task necessary to develop fluent reading skills, and require focused instruction to make up for the lost time.

Take Away ELLs do not have the oral comprehension of grammar that NES students bring with them when starting to read. The higher their grade level when entering U.S. schools, the broader the divide they have to cross to catch up to NES students. To make up for the extensive amounts of reading NES students complete every year, ELLs need focused, explicit teaching of the grammatical structures they need to know in order to comprehend their textbooks.

Reading Speed

Consider the following questions:
- How fast should students read?
- How do reading speeds differ between different types of texts?
- How can teachers help ELLs increase their reading speeds?

Silent reading speed differs depending on the difficulty, length, topic, and purpose of a given text. Reading speed for a newspaper article, for example, is typically faster than for a textbook. However, if the reader is going to be tested on the details of the article, the speed will decrease. Moreover, individuals who are fluent NES readers differ in the speed with which they read the same texts. Some people finish a novel in a few hours, while others take their time and spend hours every day to finish the same novel. However, it is generally true that increased reading speed is correlated with improved reading ability: Better readers tend to be faster readers. It may be that with NES readers there is a point of diminishing returns, so that the reader who finishes first is not necessarily the reader who can best answer questions about the text. For ELLs, however, it is important to keep in mind that reading speed affects everything from whether or not they can finish the assigned textbook reading on time to how well they score on the exam.

Targets for silent reading speed differ depending on whether the student is engaged in light pleasure reading, reading with time constraints (such as on exams), or study reading in a textbook. The three seem to be related to the extent that if a student's pleasure reading increases, the other two will also increase. Typically, activities that are intended to increase a student's reading speed focus on the type of short timed readings found on exams. In this case, NES students score well on tests like the Scholastic Aptitude Test (SAT) if they can read at 400 words per minute (wpm). ELLs who do well on the Test of English as a Foreign Language (TOEFL) typically read such texts at more than 250 wpm. ELLs who exit ESL classes in the United States may still be reading at only 100 wpm. Study reading, when students know that they need to retain the information from the book in order to answer questions on a test later, might slow the reading speed to 25% of the light reading speed.

Imagine what that means on an exam: An NES student might read a 400-word passage in 1 minute, when an ELL in the same class takes 4 minutes to read the same text. If the NES reads and answers the typical multiple-choice question in 30 seconds, it will take the ELL 2 minutes. When the NES can read through an entire test in 20 minutes and be ready to answer questions, the ELL will take 1 hour and 20 minutes to read the same test. Whether the subject is math, science, history, or ELA, ELLs are disadvantaged by slower reading speed—even though they might know the material and be able to answer the questions, given time. Typical accommodation in schools allows for "time and a half" for the exam: clearly not sufficient for such gaps in reading rate.

Imagine a 200-page novel that has an average of 250 words on each page. The NES whose light reading speed is 400 wpm can finish the novel in 8 hours of sustained silent reading with sufficient comprehension and retention of detail to do well on a test about the book. The ELL whose light reading speed is 100 wpm will take 32 hours to read the same book. In an extensive reading program, the NES will read four books for every one book read by the advanced ELL, causing the Matthew Effect (Stanovich, 1986).

Take Away ELLs read at a lower rate than NES students. This means that they will have difficulty keeping up with homework, reading instructions in class, and finishing exams. While speed alone is not a guarantee of reading ability, it is one necessary component, and teachers in all subjects should work to improve ELL students' reading speeds.

Fluency

Consider the following questions:
- How fast do your students read?
- How much time do you allow your class to read one page? One book chapter?
- Can your ELLs finish the same assignment in the same amount of time as your NESs?
- Is it always better to read fast?
- How is it possible to know every word but not understand a text?

Reading fluency is listed as a target standard for foundational levels in reading, K–5, in the Common Core (NGA & CCSSO, 2010b). Unlike NES students, ELLs will require fluency training throughout their schooling. Grabe (2004) provides a comprehensive review of the reading fluency research, and implications for ELLs. True fluency depends on students' ability to automatically recognize and comprehend words on the text (Kuhn & Stahl, 2003). There are an estimated 30 separate activities that take place in each second of reading (Taylor, 2011). NES students whose oral skills are advanced beyond the level of the text they are reading have typically achieved a level of fluency that allows them to comprehend the text as easily as they comprehend oral language, increasing reading speed each year of school. Native English speaker reading can occur at rates (measured in words per minute) faster than one can read aloud. NES students reach an average fluent reading rate of 250 words per minute in 12th grade, where "fluency in silent reading means adequate reading rate, good comprehension, as well as ease and comfort in reading" (Taylor & Spichtig, 2011, p. 167).

Traditionally, ELL instruction focused on pushing students to read faster, while maintaining a certain minimum level of comprehension. However, recent studies indicate that real reading fluency is more than reading at speed with comprehension (Bar-Kochva, 2013; Breznitz, 2006; Grabe 2004; Kuhn & Stahl, 2003; Nagy, 2005). It is generally true that students who read too slowly do not comprehend the text. However, it is also true that ELLs who are asked to read faster can read each word of a text aloud and not comprehend the content of the text (Pilgreen, 2010). There seems to be a sweet spot, a range of speeds that are optimal for comprehension, dependent on the student's age and English language ability (Taylor & Spichtig, 2011), where students increase speed, comprehension, and comfort with reading simultaneously.

Take Away ELLs don't just need to read faster, they need to read more fluently. While NES students have developed a rhythm and pacing system that matches the orthography to their mental understanding of the spoken language, ELLs may not have a well-developed sense of the rhythm and flow of English.

Background Knowledge

Consider the following questions:
- What is the role of topic in reading comprehension?
- Why do some students have difficulty reading Shakespeare but not Harry Potter?
- Why do the cultural, historical, and social background of a text affect student comprehension?

Reading does not take place in a vacuum. Every text a student reads is situated within a context, or rather a variety of contexts. There is the current context of the modern classroom, where the teacher assigns a text, other students are reading the same (or similar) texts, and the ELL is expected to read and react to the text in some way. Then there is the context of the origin of the text, a writer situated in a specific historical time and place writing to a specific audience, typically one situated in the author's own time and place. Moreover, there is a different context for each reader, the knowledge that each individual brings to the text about life, human behavior, and the world around her or him. Shakespeare certainly did not write *Romeo and Juliet* for the purpose of having a 10th-grade student from China currently living in the United States understand plot development well enough to pass a state-mandated test. He did not limit his word choice to the high school word list. Providing culturally appropriate texts for students to read will help ELLs understand the U.S. educational context and how it differs from their home cultures.

The Common Core Standards note, "By reading texts in history/social studies, science, and other disciplines, students build a foundation of knowledge in these fields that will also give them the background to be better readers in all content areas" (NGA & CCSSO, 2010b, p. 10). ELLs who have not moved up through the U.S. education system have not had the exposure to this variety of texts in English. Therefore, ELLs will not have the sociocultural or linguistic knowledge needed to comprehend age-appropriate and grade-level texts in English.

In order to manage any assigned text, readers need to understand the contexts of the text and the classroom and connect them to their own knowledge and experiences. The manner of making these connections needs to be explicitly taught to ELLs. Different levels of background are needed to read novels than to read textbooks, but whether the reading is a math or science text or a play in an ELA class, some background knowledge is necessary for comprehension. Providing this knowledge will help ELLs understand the key meaning of the text.

At a minimum, ELLs need to know what the purpose of the text is, how the current reading fits into the discourse history of the topic (Why are we studying geometry now when we were studying algebra last month?), and what they are expected to do with the information once they have read the text. For example, in a 47-page chapter on finding the volume of shapes in a math textbook, how do volumes relate to the previous chapter on areas? In what real-life situations might one need to know the volume of objects? How will knowing these formulas prepare the student for algebra 2? How much do students really need to know in order to meet the state standards on the test? Perhaps the students will be tested on the formulas for six to eight shapes (spheres, cones, cylinders, cubes, pyramids, rectangular prisms)? So pointing out to the ELL the four specific pages on which these formulas are illustrated would be a useful step in the reading process: "Read enough to understand these eight formulas on these four pages. You will have to find the volumes of these shapes on the test next week and on the final exam in April."

Take Away ELLs need explicit teaching of the basic tropes and setting of a text before being asked to read. All students benefit from having an idea about what will be in a given reading before they begin to read. However, unlike NES students who may be able to quickly discern the basic formulas of English text and predict the structure and organization, ELLs may not be able to discern the text purpose and author's intent from cues in the introduction. Teaching ELLs about the content and structure of a text they are about to read will provide them with mental connections for the new information they encounter in the text.

Strategies

Consider the following questions:
- *What do you do when you see a word you do not know?*
- *How do you make sense of new grammatical constructions?*
- *How do you comprehend the following sentences?*
    1. *Sports reporter register is replete with cataphoric deixis.*
    2. *All mimsy were the borogoves, and the mome raths outgrabe.[2]*
- *What do NES students draw on to make sense of texts to which ELLs may not have access?*
- *How can teachers encourage ELLs to apply useful reading strategies to improve their comprehension of content-area textbooks?*

Clearly, not all students will learn or choose to use the same reading strategies. However, the evidence strongly indicates that all good readers do use strategies while reading in order to comprehend difficult text (August & Shanahan, 2006; Gersten et al., 2007; Manchón, 2008). Some of these strategies may be intuitive for certain students (e.g., if you see a word you don't know, read past it to see if you can comprehend the text without knowing that particular word) while others are almost certainly learned behaviors (e.g., highlighting key words). The Common Core Standards state that by Grades 11–12 students should be "choosing flexibly from a range of strategies" (NGA & CCSSO, 2010b, p. 55) to understand reading and content.

---

[2] Explanation by Lewis Carroll (1875) a.k.a. Charles Lutwidge Dodgson: "'MIMSY' is 'flimsy and miserable' (there's another portmanteau for you). And a 'BOROGOVE' is a thin shabby-looking bird with its feathers sticking out all round—something like a live mop." "And then 'MOME RATHS'?" said Alice. "I'm afraid I'm giving you a great deal of trouble." "Well, a 'RATH' is a sort of green pig: but 'MOME' I'm not certain about. I think it's short for 'from home'—meaning that they'd lost their way, you know." . . . "'OUTGRABING' is something between bellowing and whistling, with a kind of sneeze in the middle."

ELLs who enter the U.S. K–12 system beyond the third grade are not as likely to have been taught a wide range of reading strategies. Within a systematic approach to improving ELL students' reading abilities, teachers should teach a variety of reading strategies, and encourage students to use those strategies both in and outside of class. Reading strategies can focus on pre-, during-, and postreading activities, and can be silent and internal (e.g., looking at graphics in the text and thinking about what they mean), oral (e.g., sharing what you have read with a partner), or written (e.g., taking notes). The keys to successful strategy instruction are to teach the strategies in a systematic way, through modeling and having students practice them, and recycling them throughout the year as students tackle increasingly difficult texts.

ELLs may or may not have a strong academic background in their own languages. Either way, they need to learn the academic and English literacy conventions required to succeed in U.S. high schools. This includes learning reading strategies that they can use for comprehending texts, gathering information from the text, remembering the information gathered, and applying the knowledge gained to their schoolwork. This is necessary for them to be able to participate actively in class, work on projects, write papers, and take tests.

The strategies a student uses for a given text will be determined by the difficulty level of the text, the genre, the length, and the level of comprehension expected. For example, one set of strategies might be used for studying a textbook, and a different set for reading a short story. When texts appropriate to the students' home cultures and relevant to their current U.S. educational culture are assigned, teachers can demonstrate strategies for comprehension that will differ across text types. Which strategies are taught to (or learned by) the student is not as important as that they are taught regularly in a systematic manner.

Take Away Given the many differences between ELL and NES students' knowledge and use of reading strategies, teachers should provide explicit strategy instruction at all levels. Where NES students have often developed English reading strategies before they arrive at school, ELLs may not even have such strategies in their home language. Strategies based on an assumption of oral language proficiency are the most problematic for ELLs, because although they seem the simplest, they depend on oral skills that have not been taught. Unlike NES children, ELLs will not have been surrounded by English oral language, and will not have internalized abilities such as rhyming or sounding out a word.

Conclusion

For these reasons, and also because ELLs have not read widely on their own nor been read to in English, ELLs will always read more slowly than their NES peers. This in turn means that they will have trouble finishing in-class activities, including quizzes and tests. Moreover, taking more time while reading textbooks

Table 1. Key Reading Differences Between ELLs and NES Students

	ELLs	NES Students
Vocabulary	Begin with 0 words in English; can communicate in English with only 2,000 words; need at least 9,000 words to be prepared for university	Begin school with 5,000 words; will increase at least 3,000 words per year; will know more than 40,000 words when entering university
Grammar	Lack basic structures such as article and preposition use; need to learn the oral forms	Understand all oral forms of grammar; may have trouble transferring oral grammar to written forms
Strategies	Tend to apply few strategies to every reading challenge, even when they are not useful	Use a range of reading strategies depending on the reading task
Fluency	Reading lags behind oral fluency; lack prosody and rhythm while reading; read grade-level material silently slower than they can speak	Reading exceeds oral fluency can read silently at grade level faster than they speak
Background knowledge	Lack the *cultural knowledge* needed to understand literary allusions, euphemisms, and idioms	Share wide sociocultural and historical background knowledge that support reading comprehension

means that the ELL will understand less of the course material than NES students do. Because English is the medium of instruction in the United States, there is a sense in which all teachers are English teachers. Teachers need to systematically focus on teaching ELLs the vocabulary and grammar that will help them comprehend the texts in all of their classes (not just English or ESL classes). This goes beyond teaching new vocabulary found in the textbook glossary and new sentence forms that are directly connected to the content (e.g., conditional *if . . . then* sentences). In any class where teachers assign reading, they need to help ELLs build reading fluency; use before-, during-, and after-reading strategies; and work to develop ELLs' background knowledge about the assigned readings. Table 1 provides a quick visual comparison of the key reading differences between ELLs and NES students.

Sociocultural Factors and ELL Reading

4

Consider the following questions:
- *How do we define* American children*?*
- *What is the definition of* English speaker*?*
- *Are there English language learners (ELLs) who are born in the United States?*
- *When do children learn the alphabet?*
- *When do children learn to read?*
- *Whose task is it to teach beginning literacy skills?*

Effective instruction is culturally appropriate. It builds on the skills, knowledge, and experiences that students acquire prior to coming to school and while they are in school, and it extends and broadens their skills and experiences in developmentally meaningful ways throughout the 13 school years. (TESOL, 2010, p. 12)

Teachers can state with some certainty that NES students who enter their classrooms share some common cultural experiences and background knowledge in the subject being taught. For example, in fourth grade, my class studied state history (Wyoming, in my case), so when the fifth-grade social studies teacher began the unit on national parks, she could reasonably assume that we had all read that Yellowstone was the first national park in the world. Similarly, English teachers can begin the year reviewing the books that were required reading in the previous year. Teachers can also assume that in a classroom of NES students, everyone in the class can understand lectures, instructions, plays on words, and jokes at a given level. That is, fifth-grade teachers know not to use tenth-grade vocabulary to explain new concepts.

ELLs, on the other hand, come to class with a widely ranging set of cultural experiences and background knowledge. Some have had formal schooling in their home countries, while others have not. Some know the history of the Middle East from the European Judeo-Christian perspective, and others from a Semitic Muslim perspective. Some ELLs read fluently in their home language, perhaps even in several languages, while others come from an oral language background with no written form. Most ELLs stay in the school system for years, so most ELLs who enter a given classroom have had some ESL lessons. They may even have been exited from the district's ESL program and not be able to read at grade level.

It is therefore imperative that teachers learn about each student's knowledge and cultural background in order to meet the TESOL standard for culturally appropriate teaching. For example, if an ELL is a Spanish speaker, she or he will know the Roman alphabet and will know many cognate words. In fact, what we think of as *difficult scientific* words (which tend to be Latinate) will be easier for Spanish speakers to understand than the *easy daily* words (which tend to be Germanic). On the other hand, students whose home language is written in a different script, such as Chinese or Arabic, will have no such advantage.

Take Away Content-area teachers are familiar with standards in their own areas, whether math, science, English language arts (ELA), or some other subject. However, many administrators and teachers are not familiar with the TESOL standards for ELL instruction. In addition to language-specific standards, TESOL has listed cultural standards that need to be addressed when teaching ELLs. These standards can be met only by knowing something about each ELL's society, life experiences, and educational background.

As mentioned earlier in this book, it is easy to fall into the trap of thinking of the issue of language in dichotomies, to assume that children either can read or they cannot, are NES or ELLs, are Americans or immigrants, know U.S. culture or do not. However, the reality is far different. Examine the scores on any state's English test and you will see that NES students in the United States demonstrate a wide range of reading ability levels, as do students labeled as ELLs. Literacy volunteers across the country will tell you that there are NES adults who remain illiterate. On the other hand, there are ELLs in the United States whose ability to read in English is above their grade level, but who are illiterate in their home languages.

Ability vs. Expectations

Language ability and the related concept of reading ability fall on continua, starting at true 0 with no defined upper limit. Readers of this text are likely to be at true 0 for language ability in Ute, a Native American language with fewer than 10 native speakers remaining. ELLs might begin school at level 0, if they have recently arrived in the United States from a country where English is not widely taught and their family does not speak it. However, ELLs do not remain at level 0 long, as they are surrounded by English and will begin to learn the language shortly after arrival in the United States. There are also many ELLs who come to the United States having studied English in their home countries, and so having achieved the ability to communicate in English. Among a group of ELLs in ninth grade, ability levels might range from true 0 to functionally bilingual.

The concept of reading *at grade level* is based on a standard bell curve. Students in the middle are *at,* those scoring significantly above the mean are *above,* and those scoring significantly below the mean are *below* grade level. In the United States, it is a societal expectation that students will enter school with some knowledge of print. Their parents have read to them at home, and they come to kindergarten understanding at least how books work. There are cultures, however, where parents do not teach children to read at home: The expectation is that schools will teach the children everything they need to know. An examination of the state standardized test scores will show that these ELLs are at a disadvantage in every field. As a whole, the group of ELLs will have lower scores on math, science, and history, not just ELA. However, it is not true that the highest ELL score will fall short of the lowest NES score. The term *limited English proficiency* fell out of use because it was an insufficient description of the students. In fact, many U.S. NES students have limited English proficiency, as shown by the number of them who are not reading at grade level. On the other hand, there are ELLs who read at grade-level proficiency or above. NES students share some of the characteristics that make it hard for ELLs to read. However, ELLs are more likely to have gaps in their sociocultural and historical knowledge that prevent them from fully comprehending English texts.

Cultural Affiliation

The Common Core Standards state "Students who are college and career ready in reading, writing, speaking, listening, and language . . . come to understand other perspectives and cultures" (NGA & CCSSO, 2010b, p. 7) and encourage "extensive reading of stories, dramas, poems, and myths from diverse cultures" (p. 10). Therefore, teachers should view the diversity that ELLs bring to their classes not as a deficit but as an opportunity to help NES students meet the standards. Interactive conversations between ELLs and their NES peers can help all students learn that people "from often widely divergent cultures and who represent diverse experiences and perspectives must learn and work together" (p. 7). However, self-reported cultural affiliation is not a simple "check the box" duality. A student who is born in the United States of parents from another country may associate with either culture, or with both. For example, an English teacher born in California of Mexican descent who has never lived in Mexico may alternately identify as Mexican, American, or Mexican-American. There are also many Americans, including many ELLs, whose heritage is not a simple duality. The reader may recall discussions of whether Tiger Woods is more Thai or African American, and his self-identification using the invented blend word *cablinasian* (Lind, 1998).

In the United States today, one's home culture is not necessarily fixed, but self-chosen and often fluid.

Cultural affiliation also does not accurately predict English language ability. ELLs may choose to report their home language as English, even when their dominant language ability is something else. This is one reason that depending on home language surveys for placing students into ESL classes is not in compliance with current federal statutes. For example, in the case of the Boston public schools (Zehr, 2010), the settlement states that the Boston public schools must "require a valid and reliable English proficiency assessment if the Home Language Survey (HLS) indicates that a language other than English is spoken at home or by the student, *or there is any other reason to believe the student is not proficient in English* [emphasis added]" (p. 10, point 27. b). It is also the case that self-identifying in a particular group does not necessarily mean that a student shares all of the sociocultural and historical information commonly known to her or his age cohort.

Take Away The plurality of cultural heritages within the United States, especially among the ELL population, means that students often do not share the cultural background knowledge of the author they are reading. Nevertheless, when students are not reading at grade level, it is important for them to have some idea of the meaning of cultural references they will find in the text.

Background Knowledge

Consider the following questions:
- *Who is Uncle Sam?*
- *When will pigs fly?*

One key area where cultural differences cause reading difficulty for ELLs is in background knowledge. To read the blog *Homer Simpson's Perfect Car Comes to Life at 24 Hours of LeMons* (Preston, 2013), students must understand that Homer Simpson is a cartoon character on a long-running U.S. cartoon, and that *lemon* (LeMons) is a term for a car that has major mechanical problems if they are to understand the text.

Some of this background knowledge is specifically linguistic: For example, speakers of Spanish will be familiar with the Roman alphabet when entering school, while Arabic speakers will not. However, much of the background knowledge needed is nonlinguistic. It includes various types of information that a child has picked up through the years from parents, friends, television, games, and books. Even in the United States, students do not receive exactly the same knowledge base in every school, so ELLs coming to the United States from a variety of countries will bring with them a wide range of background knowledge that will differ depending on their home culture, religion, socioeconomic status, and family history. Imagine the difference in background knowledge brought to school by a student from a small town in Arizona and a student who grew up in New York. Take the example of ELLs whose first language is Chinese: The child of a diplomat from China will have quite a different knowledge base from a child from Singapore whose parents came to the United States for graduate school. China is still a monolingual country, where use of other languages, including English, is fairly rare, while Singapore has a long tradition of multilingualism, with English abundantly present in print (including newspapers), radio, and television. What the two students know about the world will be quite different.

When discussing reading, background knowledge is important because what the reader brings into a given text colors what he or she will comprehend and take from the text. English textbooks often contain references to ideas that are "common knowledge" and literary allusions. While not central to the teaching point the author is trying to make, these literary devices are meant to be illustrative, providing the reader with connections between their prior knowledge and the new information being provided by the author. NES students might benefit from these digressions from the main teaching point. On the other hand, ELLs, who often do not share the author's background, can instead be confused by them.

Take Away ELLs often do not bring the same knowledge to school readings that NES students do because they do not have the same background. Moreover, the background knowledge brought to the classroom by ELLs is as diverse as the students themselves.

Cultural Capital

Consider the following questions:
- A reading refers to people who "expect CSI technology"; a teacher remarks, "Elementary my dear Watson!" How would an ELL understand these?
- What is the Midas touch?
- Why are people looking for the silver bullet?
- When do NES children learn that Homer means more than a cartoon character?
- What culturally situated comments in your textbook might prove puzzling for your ELLs?

Having been immersed in the culture (music, television, movies), NES students have an intuitive grasp of historical tropes and literary allusion used in textbooks. They will have been exposed to standard genres of text, including textbooks, short stories, novels, poetry, newspaper and magazine articles, and web articles. ELLs will have had far less exposure to cultural aspects of text, and a narrower range of genres.

Hirsch, Kett, and Trefil (1988) introduced the concept of cultural literacy: A wide range of ideas and concepts that form a kind of shared knowledge base in the United States; the things "everybody knows." For example, quotes from Shakespeare such as "All's well that ends well" and "at one fell swoop" abound in popular culture in conversation, movies, television shows, and popular music. Phrases like "No shit, Sherlock" and "No duh, Einstein" are part of the language of pop culture, used by people who never read Sir Arthur Conan Doyle, or who have never studied the theory of relativity. Certain ideas pervade the culture to such an extent that references to them are inserted into books with no explanation. It is taken for granted that the reader will know why the congressman went to bat for blue-collar workers, whether he struck out or hit a home run.

It is important to recognize that ELLs need to be explicitly taught the culturally bound references and expressions found in textbooks if they are to learn to read at grade level. Common sources for U.S. cultural capital include Shakespeare, sports (especially baseball, basketball, and football), literature, comic books, the Bible, movies, and television programs. ELLs have their own cultural capital. Their sports metaphors may be more soccer or cricket than baseball and football, their common quotes more from Sun Tzu or Cervantes than Shakespeare, and it is also important to acknowledge and value this cultural diversity in the school system. However, to be able to understand the required reading, it is important to gain the cultural capital that the author is using while writing the book.

Take Away The subject of a book is not the only material ELLs need to understand in order to master reading. They must also develop their cultural capital in order to comprehend culturally-bound references and examples that are widely used by authors in English.

Culture of School

Consider the following questions:
- *When students open their books to page x, should they read or listen?*
- *When is it wrong to read?*
- *Are there any books that students should not read in school?*

School has its own culture and behavioral norms. The longer an ELL has spent in the United States classroom, the more she or he will understand about our school culture. NES students entering school are taught the norms of behavior regarding books and reading. There are books one should read in school and books one should not. There are times when one may read aloud and times when silence is expected. At times, going to the bookshelf to get a dictionary while reading is acceptable, but at other times, students are expected to sit quietly at their desks. When reading some books, students can raise their hands and receive help from the teacher. When reading others, they can ask a classmate questions. These are all learned behaviors that ELLs have to be taught, and they are based on the unique culture of a given school or classroom.

NES students have spent an apprenticeship in learning. Each year they have spent in school has taught them a nuanced set of rules, attitudes, and behavioral norms that are learned behavior. Students need to learn what is acceptable at home or on the playground may not be acceptable in school. Depending on the age of the ELL entering a new school, they will face different challenges. Younger children are more closely monitored and are more likely to be told school rules explicitly, because their NES peers are also still learning. In high school, ELLs are more likely to face difficulties because the school rules are often unwritten and expected to be implicit.

Take Away School has a culture all its own, but schools in different countries do not share one set culture. Even NES children need to learn the culture of the classroom when they start school. ELLs may need to unlearn prior classroom cultural expectations before they can understand those of the new school.

Conclusion

Basic differences exist between NES readers and English language learning readers. While first-grade NES students will have a working vocabulary of more than 5,000 words, ELLs newly exited from ESL programs may have control of fewer than 2,000 words of communicative vocabulary. Moreover, the NES students will have automaticity in the use of function words such as articles and prepositions, something ELLs may never acquire, especially if they arrive after the age of puberty. NES students have also been exposed to literature, and will have a grasp of poetic phrasing and metaphor, which ELLs typically only understand in their first language. NES students will have been exposed to the idea of expository prose, and will have read books in every subject area, while ELLs just exited from ESL classes will probably not have read an entire book in English. It is necessary to address these differences explicitly across the curriculum to provide ELLs with an education equal to that received by their NES peers.

Recommendations for Practice and Strategies

5

Consider the following questions:
- *How do teachers know what level of English ability their English language learners (ELLs) have?*
- *Given that ELLs need to build their English reading abilities in order to learn from their content-area textbooks, who is responsible for helping them?*
- *Who teaches reading in your school?*

ELLs face an uphill battle to catch up to age-appropriate reading levels as the bar is raised each year. It has become clear that the reason ELLs continue to fall behind is that U.S. schools are not addressing their needs in a sufficient way (U.S. Department of Education, 2013). Many districts hire part-time ESL instructors, or split ESL teachers' time between several schools within the district. Some districts place ELLs under the instruction of the reading specialist or the special education teacher. However, what is really needed is a comprehensive approach to teaching ELLs to read in every class in every subject (NGA & CCSSO, 2010b). All teachers need to be English teachers because English is the medium of instruction in U.S. schools.

TESOL professionals advocate a process of building English proficiency through direct instruction and scaffolded learning across the curriculum (Echevarria, Vogt, & Short, 2004; Fillmore & Snow, 2000; Nagy, 2005). Not every teacher can be a highly trained specialist in ESL instruction, but every teacher can learn a few basic skills and strategies that will help support ELLs in learning English. The Common Core Standards clearly call for all teachers to focus on improving students' language in all four language skills (listening, speaking, reading, and writing; NGA & CCSSO, 2010b). However, ELLs will require more language support than native-English-speaking (NES) students, especially in the core area of reading. The purpose of this book is to provide specific techniques that educators working with ELLs can use to address the specific needs of their students. Table 2 presents a summary of learning needs of ELL vs. NES students.

Building Vocabulary

Consider the following questions:

- How many words do students need to learn each year?
- How many words to ELLs need to learn to catch up to their peers at various grade levels?
- What words do students need to know to read a fifth-grade math textbook?
- How do teachers know which words to teach if they are not in the textbook glossary?
- How do students know which words to study?
- How can all teachers incorporate the teaching of a wide range of vocabulary?

Vocabulary development may be the area most in need of support in every content area (Schmitt, Jiang, & Grabe, 2011). In the Common Core, the vocabulary standards "focus on understanding words and phrases, their relationships, and their nuances and on acquiring new vocabulary, particularly general

Table 2. Learning Needs of ELL vs. NES Students

	ELLs	NES Students
Building Vocabulary	Require direct instruction of Tier 1 and Tier 2 vocabulary, combining receptive and productive skills	Can learn new Tier 1 and Tier 2 vocabulary receptively, by reading
Expanding Grammar	Require direct instruction of complex English sentence patterns, phrase formation, and affix system	Can understand English sentence patterns, basic phrase structures, and affix structures; ready to learn how to write those forms
Improving Fluency	Need extensive practice in reading and listening to English to develop a sense of rhythm and fluency	Fluent in spoken English, and can apply that knowledge to reading at grade level
Practicing Strategies	Need direct instruction of strategies that they can apply systematically to reading	May be able to add new reading strategies to those previously taught without direct instruction

academic and domain-specific words and phrases" (NGA & CCSSO, 2010a, p. 8). But which and how many words?

Most teachers recognize that they are teaching students new vocabulary, but few teachers recognize how many new words students in U.S. schools are expected to learn each year (3,000 according to Stahl, 1999) in order to be successful. Often, teachers explicitly address only the vocabulary listed in the glossaries of their textbooks. It is expected that if a student has reached a given grade level, the student must know the vocabulary used by the textbook authors at that level. This is a fallacy even for U.S. NES students, and causes proportionally larger problems for ELLs, slow readers, and special needs students. Not addressing grade-level vocabulary in a systematic manner across all content areas does in fact leave some children behind.

However, learning a few basic facts about vocabulary and applying those facts to direct instruction within the classroom can help teachers to build students' knowledge base and corresponding ability to read and comprehend texts (Snow & Kim, 2007). In K–12 schools, the typical situation is that ELLs receive 1 hour a day of English language instruction. Imagine if instead they could receive systematic vocabulary instruction from five or six teachers every day. If the vocabulary surrounding the core content is taught as a regular part of their classes, their reading ability will become more fluent and reading homework will become less frustrating (NGA & CCSSO, 2010d). By incorporating targeted vocabulary instruction in all content areas, school districts should see a gradual improvement of reading ability, which has been shown to correlate to improvement on all content-area test scores (Stanovich, 2000).

The question of what vocabulary to study is not an easy one. Many variables affect vocabulary acquisition, such as student age, reading ability in the first language, amount of exposure to English in daily life, motivation, and individual learning style. So how does the individual teacher choose vocabulary for ELLs to learn? There are some common methods of choosing vocabulary targets that work for a wide variety of students. These strategies and techniques are based on a few basic rules of thumb derived from the research (Grabe, 2009; Nagy, 2005; Stahl, 1999).

1. More common words should be learned before studying less common ones.

2. Words should be studied in context.

3. Visual cues, such as pictures and models, help students learn and retain new words.

4. Definitions for new words should be simple and should use only words the student already knows.

5. Repetition of new words in meaningful ways aids in memory.

6. New words should be introduced using all four skills: reading, writing, listening, and speaking.

7. Explicitly teaching word families helps students expand their vocabulary and improve their grammar.

8. Collocations—words that are frequently found together—should be explicitly taught (e.g., black and white; traffic jam).

Word Lists

Having lists of suggested vocabulary items can provide administrators and teachers with a source of items to test. Including frequently used words on regular vocabulary quizzes or tests alongside content vocabulary from textbook glossaries can signal to teachers and students that there is a set of age- and level-appropriate vocabulary items to learn. It provides an ongoing set of goals toward which the entire learning community can work. Individual students can refer to the list to work at their own pace, using learning strategies that work best for them.

The Common Core Standards require a renewed focus on vocabulary teaching and learning. Addressing what is seen as a limitation of previous curricula, the Standards note that:

> The importance of students acquiring a rich and varied vocabulary cannot be overstated. Vocabulary has been empirically connected to reading comprehension since at least 1925 (Whipple, 1925) and had its importance to comprehension confirmed in recent years (National Institute of Child Health and Human Development, 2000). It is widely accepted among researchers that the difference in students' vocabulary levels is a key factor in disparities in academic achievement (Baumann & Kameenui, 1991; Becker, 1977; Stanovich, 1986), but that vocabulary instruction has been neither frequent nor systematic in most schools (Biemiller, 2001; Durkin, 1978; Lesaux, Kieffer, Faller, & Kelley, 2010; Scott & Nagy, 1997). (NGA & CCSSO, 2010c, p. 32)

They suggest a list of target vocabulary words for NES students at each level (K–12), and for every content area (NGA & CCSSO, 2010a), and emphasize that teachers in every subject need to focus on building students' vocabulary. ELLs will need a list of core words that is much shorter than that of their NES peers, such as the BNL (Neufeld & Billuroğlu, 2006). The older the student on entering the U.S. school system, the harder it will be to catch up.

Often, ELLs struggle with content not because they have difficulty with science or math concepts, but because they struggle to understand the language surrounding those concepts. A primary reason for this is that few content-area teachers keep in mind that ELLs do not know the same vocabulary as NES students. Schools should choose a word list for ELLs (e.g., the BNL) and provide copies of the list to all of the stakeholders. The list should be divided into levels that work within the local curriculum. This will ensure that administrators, teachers, and students are on the same page in the area of vocabulary. Agreeing on lists of words to target and test at each grade level provides a useful cohesive device for the school as a whole. Administrators can refer to the lists when choosing which textbooks to buy, what words might need to be included in supplemental activities, and which words should be used when writing content tests.[3] Teachers can use the lists to teach new vocabulary in a systematic way across the semester. Students can use lists to self-assess their progress toward their target reading goals. Administrators can use the lists to track students' progress toward college preparedness.

ELLs might be able to understand math concepts but be unable to read textbooks and materials at the same level. For example, students who can solve math problems written only with numbers might struggle to solve the same problem when it is written in sentence or paragraph format—even U.S. NES children struggle with story problems. Therefore, everyone who works with ELLs should recognize that there is a difference between the level of age-appropriate content and the level of grade-related vocabulary students can understand. Vocabulary lists allow teachers to scaffold (Vygotsky, 1978) instruction by creating supplemental materials that are written at a level of comprehensible input (Krashen, 1981), so that students do not have to struggle with reading those materials. This in turn allows students to focus more of their cognitive attention on the content of the materials and less on puzzling out the meanings of unknown words in the text.

The BNL list does not include all of the vocabulary known by a typical university freshman. Rather, it is meant to be an elemental list of the most common words that ELLs should know when they graduate from a U.S. high school. In other words, by ensuring that ELLs know the majority of the words on the BNL list, teachers make it possible for those students to continue to read and learn beyond graduation, increasing their chances of entering college. Within a given school or program, the list can be broken down into manageable chunks, providing benchmarks for vocabulary every year, semester, or month.

Take Away All students benefit from a systematic approach to direct instruction of vocabulary. ELLs in particular require some such organizing principle in order to catch up to their NES peers. The system can be based on published vocabulary lists, but it is important that basic vocabulary, not just the difficult academic vocabulary, be included on the list. Lists prepared for NES students are too advanced for ELLs and may produce unrealistic expectations, so a list targeted at ELL populations should be chosen.

---

[3] Test item stems and choices should use language that students already know. For example, a seventh grade math test should use language that students were taught in the fifth grade, unless the purpose is to test new vocabulary. Using vocabulary being taught at the current grade level imposes a double cognitive burden. It is essentially testing two subjects with one item. It would be unclear whether students missed the item because they don't know the math or because they don't understand the English. ELLs should receive tests that carefully control the English language to a level they have mastered.

Dictionaries and Dictionary Use

Consider the following questions:

- *When recently arrived ELLs don't know the alphabet thoroughly, how do they look words up in the dictionary?*
- *Have you ever looked up one word in the dictionary only to find three words in the definition that you don't know?*
- *How can K–12 educators scaffold dictionary use for ELLs to support student learning of vocabulary to catch them up to their NES peers?*

ELLs need to develop the skills to become independent readers. One of the keys to independence is the ability to learn language from the text. This in turn indicates the need for students to be able to learn the meanings of words they encounter when there is insufficient contextual support to guess. Dictionaries are the main resource students have to expand vocabulary when reading independently.

The Common Core Standards (NGA & CCSSO, 2010a) list use of dictionaries as a target skill for students in every level beginning in Grade 2. Unfortunately, standard U.S. dictionaries that are intended for NES students are not particularly useful to ELLs. Word definitions written with the assumption that children have an NES vocabulary are often ambiguous. Frequently, such definitions contain words that an ELL does not understand. This means that looking words up in the typical classroom dictionary can lead to frustration rather than to learning.

There are, however, excellent resources to help ELLs learn new words even when they do not have the first 5,000-word vocabulary expected of U.S. students entering elementary school. Picture dictionaries, such as those produced by Oxford University Press and Longman allow students to find words by category using images, or to look up images that define new words (for example, the Merriam Webster, 2014, Visual Dictionary Online at http://www.visualdictionary online.com/) Typical picture dictionaries contain around 5,000 of the most frequent words, enough to get ELLs started reading. There are also bilingual dictionaries based on Spanish, Arabic, and other languages. Increasingly, good picture dictionaries are appearing online (see Online Resources below).

Once ELLs get beyond the vocabulary of the picture dictionaries, and have a basic vocabulary of more than 2,000 words, there are several choices of learner's dictionaries to support their reading. Learner's dictionaries typically have tens of thousands of entries, but the definitions for each word are limited to a basic set of vocabulary items. For example, Longman's *Dictionary of Contemporary English* (2014) uses the 2,000 most common words in their definitions. The *Oxford Advanced Learner's Dictionary* (2014) uses the Oxford 3,000 keywords. Both of these dictionaries can be easily accessed online. Limiting the definition vocabulary means that ELLs don't get frustrated in a circular chase to define words found in the definitions of other words.

Target Vocabulary

Consider the following questions:

- *Are some words on the target list more important than others to teach?*
- *How do educators choose which vocabulary words to teach to ELLs in their content-area lessons?*
- *How do teachers categorize words on their target vocabulary lists?*
- *How can teachers differentiate vocabulary for ELLs from vocabulary for NES students?*

Although estimates vary, according to both the Google/Harvard analysis (Michel et al., 2011) and The Global Language Monitor, as of 2009 there are more than 1,000,000 words in the English lexicon. No individual could know all of these words. In fact, it is estimated that the average college graduate in the United States knows approximately 60,000 active and 73,000 passive words (Stahl, 1999). Clearly some of these words are more useful than others.

When choosing words to be targeted for teaching ELLs on an organizational level, it is important to keep in mind that the goal is not to match the vocabulary of native speakers, but to provide the vocabulary necessary so that the ELL can keep up in content-area classes. In order to choose the best words to target, I recommend focusing on frequency, productivity, and need (e.g., how many times does a student in the United States need the word *aardvark*?).

The words that children learn growing up are those that they encounter most frequently. The individual's known vocabulary can be idiosyncratic based on parents' work, hobbies, and interests; what television shows and movies they watch; and what children's books they buy. Therefore, while NES students know around 5,000 words of vocabulary when entering school, those won't be the exact same words known by every other NES child. Estimates of vocabulary ELLs need for basic communication vary, but tend to include the 2,000 most frequent words in any language (e.g., personal pronouns and words for meeting basic needs like food and clothing; Council of Europe, 2011). The Common Core Standards recognize that "each grade will include students who are still acquiring English. For those students, it is possible to meet the standards in reading, writing, speaking, and listening without displaying native-like control of conventions and vocabulary" (NGA & CCSSO, 2010b, p. 6).

If ELLs entering the school system are taught the most frequent words first, they will have a better knowledge base when they begin to read. Remember that these most frequent words are mostly Tier 1, with some Tier 2 items (Beck & McKeown, 1985; Beck, McKeown, & Omanson, 1987). Ideally, after ELLs have mastered the majority of these words, they can begin to learn the Tier 2 and 3 words needed to read and understand academic textbooks.

"Productivity" refers to the usefulness of a given word. Words that are not in the high-frequency list will be more useful to students if they are words that are used in many language domains. For example, the words for numbers (e.g., one, two, first, second) are not necessarily in the highest frequency category (partly because the actual number is more common in text than the spelled-out word). However, numbers are needed daily, and should be taught orally to newly arrived ELLs. In high school, *percent* and its affiliated words (e.g., *percentage, percentile*) are not high frequency, but their use in school across all content areas might make them more salient to teach than *sum*, which is most often found in math textbooks at the lower levels. Typically, Tier 2 words are more productive than Tier 3 words.

The need for a given word will vary depending on circumstances. When beginning to teach the Tier 1 words to a child who has just arrived in the United States, it is important to keep in mind that the words of the here-and-now can be learned most easily. For example, teachers can begin by teaching nouns referring to items in the classroom, and verbs for daily school activities (Popko, 2014). Immediate need for a given word should trump considerations of frequency in the wider community.

A student who is studying science this semester needs *periodic table* in order to understand the reading and homework, and to pass the test, no matter where in the United States the school is. That the term is not needed in daily conversation or in any other content area does not negate the need to teach it. Other Tier 3 words are not equally important in every school. In many states, required exams include the vocabulary of local geography, so that younger students may need *peninsula* for the tests in Florida and Michigan, while the same age group may not need that word in Montana or Arizona.

All teachers teach new vocabulary. They use many teaching strategies in their classes already. However, given that ELLs need to have Tier 1 and 2 words explicitly taught, it is necessary for most teachers to expand their vocabulary teaching activities once an ELL has entered their classrooms. Vocabulary that NES students have already mastered will need to be explicitly taught to ELLs at the same grade level. A quick analysis of the text you are planning to use in class can help determine the level of vocabulary needed to read the passage. If the ELL students' approximate vocabulary levels are known as well, the teacher can create some form of accommodation for the students. This might include simplifying the text in advance, preteaching words that are above the students' levels, or choosing a different text to present the same information.

Determining an individual ELL's target vocabulary requires awareness of the student's current vocabulary knowledge and its relationship to the language in the textbooks and materials to be covered in a given class. If the school has a leveled list of target vocabulary for ELLs, the teacher can create quick needs assessments to measure an individual ELL's word knowledge. Create a simple MC or fill-in assessment using a random set of words from the list at the level appropriate to the age cohort and each level below it. For example, if your class materials use many of your level 3 words, but not many at higher levels, create the assessment from words at levels 1, 2, and 3. If your materials use many words at level 6, the assessment should instead use levels 4, 5, and 6.

Take Away Word lists for ELLs can be useful tools for meeting target learning standards. They should be largely similar across time and geography, but should be adapted to specific teaching situations through analyses of the reading that a given school requires. The most common and useful words (Tier 1) should be taught to all ELLs prior to reading instruction. Tier 2 highly productive words can be taught to complement reading instruction throughout the student's school years. Tier 3 words should be taught within each content area as needed. Vocabulary instruction should be individualized to each ELL, given the wide range of base knowledge each student brings to bear on reading.

Expanding Grammar

Consider the following questions:
- *What role does grammar play in the structuring of information presented in content textbooks?*
- *How does the grammar complexity of texts increase across the 12 years a student is in school?*
- *What is the role of grammar in reading comprehension?*
- *How can teachers scaffold reading for ELLs by paying attention to grammar?*

Understanding grammar is an integral part of knowing a language. NES students grow up surrounded by the language, and internalize the grammar of English most prevalent in their surroundings. Although grammar might at first appear to be a culturally neutral issue, the grammar chosen by a given writer is in fact culturally embedded. For example, children in any of the areas where the Southern American accent is spoken will naturally use the term *ya'll*—though there are a variety of forms of this term depending on geographic region. In eastern Canada, children are accustomed to adding *eh* to the end of sentences. Similarly, all native speakers of English will grow up having acquired all of the basic grammar of English. NES children use subject–verb–object (SVO) sentence patterning (as compared to Japanese, for example, which uses subject–object–verb). They will also have mastered articles and prepositions, grammar forms not found in many languages. However, details within these conventions will differ by language community: U.S. children stand *in line* while British children stand *on line*. ELLs do not have this advantage of beginning to read English with a subconscious knowledge of the way the language fits together (Barone & Xu, 2008; Genesee et al., 2006), so teaching them the conventions using culturally appropriate materials is beneficial. It is important to use texts appropriate to the U.S. educational culture, but also those texts that use language with which ELLs are more familiar.

Grammar means the structure of language, including formation of word forms, such as verb tenses (by adding suffixes) and the order of words within a sentence. Note that writing conventions, such as punctuation and spelling, are not actually grammar. Nor are spoken registers such as teen-speak or texting, in themselves, grammar. Many U.S. teachers complain that their NES students have poor grammar, when what they mean by this is that their students have not mastered the academic writing conventions required in the educational setting, or that their students are using informal spoken language conventions deemed inappropriate within the hallowed halls of academia. In most cases, native speaker errors in speaking and writing grammar do not interfere with their ability to understand spoken or written English. ELLs, on the other hand, need to learn grammar basics in order to be able to comprehend classroom lessons and textbooks. Therefore, this section focuses on keys to grammar rather than conventions.

Teachers can help ELLs develop grammar knowledge through targeted direct instruction. They should know the grammar of the reading they are requiring, and preteach ELLs how to make meaning from the text. However, teachers can also help ELLs develop a subconscious knowledge of grammar by patiently providing consistent language input at a level matching the students' abilities and increasing the complexity of the language they, the teachers, are using over time. Handouts, homework assignments, quizzes, tests, and assignment feedback should be consciously constructed to match ELLs' current language ability levels. If it is, ELLs can learn age- and grade-appropriate content in math, science, history, and other subject areas.

Parts of Words

English is an inflectional language (Summer Institute of Linguistics, 2003). This means that words in English consist of a root, and add affixes that can change the meaning or word class. Some ELLs come from languages (especially European languages) that have similar inflectional word-formation processes. In that case, if they are literate in their home language, they can understand the concept of analyzing a word for its root and suffixes. Other ELLs come from analytic languages like Chinese, and will need more support to understand how English works.

English has hundreds of affixes (a sample list can be found in Table 3). NES students often learn the rules for using affixes before they arrive in school through rhymes, books, and word play. They are expected to know these rules orally when they begin to read. The Common Core Standards (NGA & CCSSO, 2010b) require that in second grade students be able to "decode words with common prefixes and suffixes" (p. 16). However, they continue to learn rules and processes beyond the most common affixes throughout K–12 (e.g., –ology, dem–). Therefore, even NES students are expected to "identify and correctly use patterns of word changes that indicate different meanings or parts of speech (e.g., analyze, analysis, analytical; advocate, advocacy)" (p. 55).

Table 3. Sample List of English Affixes

Prefix	Meaning	Example
a–	without	moral → amoral
bi–	two	lingual → bilingual
co–	together	operate → cooperate
extra–	beyond, more than	curricular → extracurricular
il–, im–, in–, ir–, un–	negative	logical → illogical perfect → imperfect effective → ineffective regular → irregular able → unable
mono–	one	lingual → monolingual
non–	without	fat → nonfat
pre–	before	view → preview

Suffix	Change	Example
–ed	verb + past tense	walk → walked
–s	verb + 2nd person present singular	walk → walks
–s	noun + plural	cat → cats
–er	adjective + comparison = comparative	big → bigger
–ance	verb → noun	appear → appearance
–er	verb → personal noun	teach → teacher
–ist	object noun → personal noun	cello → cellist
–ship	personal noun → emotional noun	friend → friendship
–able	noun → adjective	comfort → comfortable
–ful	noun → adjective	success → successful
–ive	noun → adjective	expense → expensive

ELLs need explicit instruction to learn even the most common patterns, regardless of their age when beginning school in the United States. The simplest forms for ELLs to learn are those that are most regular. It is not uncommon for ELLs to use the –ing forms before mastering the past tense –ed. However, because the –ing actually marks three possible parts of speech (verb → progressive or continuous, noun → gerund, or adjective → present participle), they may overgeneralize. Especially in Latinate languages in which the subject is optional, students may use a word with –ing as both the subject and verb in their sentences. They may get confused when hearing or seeing the –ing form as an adjective.

> **Take Away** Word formation is not a simple process in English. Teachers need to be aware of the complex nature of word formation rules in English when assigning reading texts to ELLs. ELLs will master this complex system only through focused explicit teaching over many years.

Parts of Speech

Consider the following questions:
- *What are the basic parts of speech?*
- *Are "parts of speech" the same in every language?*
- *How detailed an understanding of sentence structure is necessary for students to learn from reading?*
- *How can teachers use a basic knowledge of parts of speech in English to scaffold ELLs' reading?*

Every word in English has a form, a function, and a meaning (Larsen-Freeman, 2001, 2003). Traditional grammars of English typically label eight parts of speech (word forms)[4]: noun, pronoun, verb, adjective, article, adverb, preposition, and conjunction. However, some of the parts of speech have more than one function. Knowing both the forms and the functions of words can help students understand the word's meaning. This will help build ELLs' vocabularies and comprehension of difficult texts. Step one is to know that a word is a noun (for example). Step two is to know the function of that noun in the sentence: Is it the subject? The object of the sentence? The object of a preposition? Take the word *dog*. Most textbooks place it in the category "noun" and leave it at that. NES students learn through frequent repetition, however, that the word can have different functions:

---

[4] I have seen lists with as many as 12 and as few as 5 labels. The important point, for me, is not to analyze grammar in great detail, but to find the most productive explanations to provide ELLs.

1. The dog bit the man. (subject)

2. They read the tale of the dog and the pussycat. (object of a preposition)

3. The dog's tail got caught in the fence. (modifying the noun *tail*; possessive adjective)

4. He dogged the robber to his hideout. (verb)

5. It was a three-dog night. (modifying the noun *night*; adjective)

6. After the date, she said Bob was a dog. (object of the sentence)

7. Suddenly, everyone was dog-tired. (modifying the verb *tired*; adverb)

In order for ELLs to comprehend difficult readings, they need to understand not just the forms of the words, but their functions as well. In the preceding examples, a student asked to underline the nouns might well underline every example of *dog*. If an ELL came to a teacher to ask the meaning of dog, the teacher might show a picture or explain that a dog is an animal that is a common house pet in the United States, thinking that the student's vocabulary must be very low. However, if the student asks the meaning of sentence #4, the teacher will realize that the problem stems from a common noun being used figuratively as a verb. NES students are likely to have solved this problem at a much earlier grade level than ELLs. In fact, there is such a strong underlying sense that NES students know parts of speech that the Common Core Standards (NGA & CCSSO, 2010a) do not address this aspect of language.

In order to help ELLs better understand a reading, it is useful for teachers to show them how the text is constructed. Given long and complex sentences, the key to understanding any text is to know who or what is being discussed (the subject), what action or state of being the sentence describes (the verb), and who or what is being affected (the object). It helps to break complex sentences down into simple SVO sentences. This is particularly relevant in texts that use passive voice ("The boy was followed by the dog"). Some methods of teaching ELLs how difficult texts are structured include:

- Highlighting: Mark nouns in one color and verbs in another.

- Sentence combining: Start with simple SVO sentences and show students how to connect them to make compound and complex sentences.

- Sentence dividing: Take sentences from the text and divide them into simple sentences with SVO structure.

- Summarizing: Teach ELLs to summarize each paragraph of a difficult reading in one sentence.

- Outlining: Break a difficult reading down into a clear outline that shows one chapter on one or two pages.

Sentence Complexity

Consider the following questions:
- *What are the building blocks of English sentences?*
- *How can sentence complexity interfere with reading comprehension?*
- *How can teachers differentiate instruction for ELLs by simplifying sentence structure without compromising content-area standards?*

The basic unit of meaning in any language is the word. A group of words that function together is called a phrase. When a group of words and phrases have one subject and one verb, it is a clause. Any clause that can stand alone is a sentence. Children learn language in stages, starting with individual words (e.g., mama, drink), progressing to simple sentences (e.g., papa go; doggie come), and then to more complex sentences. They learn along the way that one word can be expanded into a more descriptive phrase, (e.g., doggie → my doggie → my big black doggie). However, the language learned at home will be oral language. The disciplined *correct grammar* forms needed for academic work are taught and learned over time in school through reading and writing exercises. The older an ELL is upon arrival in the U.S. classroom, the more necessary it will be to explicitly teach creation of word forms (e.g., plural, past tense, comparative), phrase structure, clause structure, and sentence formation. Here is an example from a fifth-grade science text (Lee, 2013):

> The long, stringy flagella, connected to a hook structure, fit over a rod that rotates inside a ring attached to the bacterium. As the rod rotates, the flagella twirl around, pushing water down and behind them to thrust the bacterium forward.

Notice how grammatically complex this passage is: There are two sentences, six clauses, at least eight phrases, and 41 words. Seven words have been deleted for stylistic reasons. What is the subject of this passage? Given that there are six clauses, what are the six subjects of the clauses? What are the six verbs?

The relative difficulty level of a text, its *readability*, can be quickly checked using the Microsoft Word readability tool, which is part of the grammar and spell check (Figure 2). Notice that this passage from a fifth-grade text ranks

The long, stringy flagella, connected to a hook structure, fit over a rod that rotates inside a ring attached to the bacterium. As the rod rotates, the flagella twirl around, pushing water down and behind them to thrust the bacterium forward.

Readability Statistics

Counts	
Words	41
Characters	202
Paragraphs	1
Sentences	2
Averages	
Sentences per Paragraph	2.0
Words per Sentence	20.5
Characters per Word	4.8
Readability	
Passive Sentences	0%
Flesch Reading Ease	51.9
Flesch-Kincaid Grade Level	11.1

OK

Figure 2. Microsoft Word Readability Statistics

at Flesh-Kincaide grade 11.1 based on the complexity of the grammar and vocabulary.

Without changing the meaning or *dumbing down* the content, this passage could be rewritten to make it comprehensible to ELLs. One way to do this would be to first define the key terms *flagella, rotates, bacterium, twirl,* and *thrust.* Then break the passage into simple sentences:

1. The flagella are long and stringy.

2. The flagella are connected to a hook structure.

3. The hook structure fits over a rod.

4. The rod rotates inside a ring.

5. The ring is attached to the bacterium.

6. The flagella twirl around the rod.

7. The twirling flagella push water down and behind them.

8. Pushing the water thrusts the bacterium forward.

The complex vocabulary could also be simplified, if your intention is to teach the ELL about bacteria (e.g., stringy → like string; rotate → turn; twirl → turn;

thrusts → moves). If the purpose is in part to teach technical vocabulary for science classes, in addition to preteaching the difficult vocabulary, use it repeatedly in speaking and writing about the topic (e.g., adding the words to vocabulary journals or putting them on a word wall). An illustration would help ELLs understand the concept and reinforce the language.

> **Take Away** Language used in textbooks becomes increasingly complex across grade levels. The later in life an ELL begins to study in the United States, the more support she or he will need in order to understand the core concepts in the textbook, and also to learn the language. Awareness of the complexity of language can help teachers accommodate ELLs' language limitations as they acquire increasingly complex English structures.

Reading Speed

Consider the following questions:
- *What would be a target reading speed for your students?*
- *How can teachers encourage students to read faster?*
- *What types of texts are useful for reading speed improvement?*

Reading speed can vary greatly depending on the text and purpose for reading. When calculating the average speed, researchers typically focus on light reading of age and ability appropriate texts, like novels and short stories. A given student's reading speed will increase for light materials like comic books, magazines on topics the reader enjoys, and light informational texts like tourist brochures or product descriptions, where the reader knows something about the topic and is not attempting to learn and remember all of the points the author is making. On the other hand, when the reader is a bit unfamiliar with the topic, and is looking for complete comprehension of the text (e.g., because there will be a quiz or test on the details), reading speed will decrease. Information density, knowledge of the subject, sentence complexity, and vocabulary level all impact the difficulty of the text. More difficult texts impose a higher cognitive load on the readers, slowing them down.

The targets at each grade level for ELLs should be set based on grade-level averages for their NES peers. Younger students do not read as quickly as older students. In the first grade, children typically read fewer than 60 words per minute (wpm), while reading rates set for high school seniors is around 400 wpm. Young ELLs will start with one word at a time, but middle school students should work toward a 100 wpm rate. By 12th grade, the target reading speed for ELLs is around 250 wpm for pleasure reading (see Taylor & Spichtig, 2011,

Table 1, p. 167). Study reading speed of informational texts for information that needs to be retained for a quiz or test will be lower than this. Quick reading of easy texts to gain the gist of the story or information should be higher.

Take Away Reading faster is generally equated with reading better, although there is a point of diminishing returns. Younger students typically read more slowly than older students. ELLs who are literate in their home language will almost certainly be reading more slowly in English than they do in their home languages. Also, ELLs' reading speeds in English will on average lag behind their NES peers. Implicit learning through extensive reading can improve reading speeds. However, explicit instruction is required for ELLs to catch up to the reading speeds of their NES peers.

Extensive Reading to Increase Reading Rate

Increasing reading speed is an important goal in itself. There are two means of increasing reading speed. The first is extensive reading (mentioned elsewhere in this book). Encouraging the student to read a large number of books at the student's comfort and ability level can motivate the student to read faster. The goal of extensive reading should be reading in itself, without required exams or expectations of academic analysis. It would be counterproductive to try to use an extensive reading activity to force students to attempt materials that are too difficult, that contain uninteresting material, or that have to be learned for a test.

Extensive reading journals allow for personalized instruction, in that students can read books that they enjoy at their own difficulty level. For extensive reading in general and when utilizing extensive reading journals, students should pick their own books (perhaps from a preselected set chosen by the teacher), and books should be high interest, at a level of easy reading comprehension, and culturally appropriate for each student. For ELLs, the books should be chosen on actual reading ability level, not based on age or current class level. If the student feels confident and would like a challenge, the book should be no more than one level higher than the current reading ability level. If the student lacks confidence and wishes to read easier books, the range should be no lower than two grades below her or his current ability level. In other words, teachers should provide books for an ELL who is reading on a fifth-grade level that range from third to sixth grade difficulty (regardless of the student's age or grade level).

The choice of books should be confidential so that the activity doesn't become a contest between students to read the most difficult book. It is counterproductive to have ELLs attempting to compete with NES readers. This can be more easily accomplished with today's technology, as students can have access to thousands of books on one e-reader. Apps such as Scholastic's *Reading Timer* can also support extensive reading journals by tracking student reading minutes.

Students should be asked to read every day. They should keep track of the amount of time they spend reading and how many pages they have read. The journal can also have a place to write a brief summary or reaction to the day's reading. Finishing a book should be marked in some way as a milestone. With younger learners, there might be a gold star. For older learners, the teacher might write a note of congratulation that the student can share with his or her parents.

Take Away Read. Analogies from sports, music, and art abound in literature: Excellence requires not just study, but also long periods of practice. If a student wants to read faster, the student needs to read a lot. Not just several pages or chapters, but lots and lots of books. Extensive reading of books ELLs enjoy builds the foundation in reading speed they need when they begin to read academic texts.

Intensive Reading

The second method for increasing reading speed is to use intensive timed reading activities with short texts in class. Having students chart their own reading speeds on short texts at levels at or slightly below their reading ability levels can help students measure their own accomplishments. Timed readings train student eye movement and focus of attention. Regular timed reading tasks push students to read faster with basic comprehension. Each reading should be followed by a few (5–10) comprehension questions. A student should be able to answer with 70–80% accuracy. If accuracy is less than 70%, the student can slow down a bit and concentrate on catching the key information. If accuracy is above 80%, the student should push to read the next passage faster.

Reading speed is gauged by the amount of material read with comprehension in a set period of time. It is typically calculated as the number of words read per minute. For example, given a 500-word text, the student who finishes in 5 minutes has a reading speed of $500 \div 5 = 100$ wpm. If a student can finish in 2 minutes, the number is $500 \div 2 = 250$ wpm, an average reading speed for 12th grade students (Taylor & Spichtig, 2011). It can also be measured in the number of pages read per hour, given that there are an average number of words per page in any given book. Students can keep this simple calculation in an ongoing timed reading journal to measure personal progress.

In an ESL class, short (400–600 word) passages with multiple-choice questions can be used to push students to read faster with comprehension. The assumption is that all students in the class fall within a reasonable range of reading ability and reading speed. With NES students, the teacher can pick short passages about the subject area (e.g., the text boxes in many textbooks include interesting biographies or stories related to the chapter topic). With ELLs, it is important to choose passages that are not too difficult. Grade-level textbooks will contain too many unknown words and complex sentences that prevent reading quickly. It is also important to use texts that are culturally appropriate and not in any way controversial. Controversial texts may slow down students' reading speed.

Given a whole class with a similar range of reading speeds and texts that are comprehensible to the students, there is a quick activity (10 minutes) that can increase reading speed over time. For this activity, all students have to begin at once as the teacher keeps time. The teacher can use a stopwatch or any watch that marks seconds.

1. Distribute the text to students, telling them not to begin until told.

2. Tell the students "Go!" and start timing.

3. As students read, the teacher marks the time on the board, noting every 6 seconds (or 1/10 of a minute), and beginning a new row for each minute:

   1. 1   2   3   4   5   6   7   8   9

   2. 1   2   3   4   5   6   7 . . .

4. When a student is finished she or he looks at the time and writes it on the paper (e.g., 2.6 or 3.5).

5. The teacher can stop once all students have finished, or at a predetermined maximum time (e.g., 4 minutes for a 400-word text).

6. Tell students the text length, and each student can do the math (e.g., 400 words ÷ 3.5 minutes = 114 wpm).

7. Students then answer the questions.

8. The teacher gives the correct answers.

9. Students chart their time and the number correct.

If students comprehend everything, they should be encouraged to increase their speed. If they score too low, they need to slow down a bit and comprehend more. For ELLs, the target should be around 75% accuracy with speed increasing over time (toward the 250 wpm mentioned earlier). NES students should work toward a higher speed, such as 400 wpm.

If an individualized program of intensive reading is needed, students can be taught to keep a reading journal on their own by using published materials (see Spargo's series of leveled timed reading texts, 2001). MacMillan has a series of timed reading books in the content areas that can also be useful for ELLs, given that the teacher is careful to choose readings by ability level rather than age of the student.

Increasingly, there are timed reading activities available for electronic media. For example, there is a series of 24 timed readings accompanying *E-Learning Companion: Student's Guide to Online Success, 4th Edition* (Watkins & Corry, 2014), which has a timed reading activity online. Apps such as Instone Software's *QuickReader: eBook Reader With Speed Reading* and Brainglass's *Read4English* can be easily adapted for ELL use at a variety of ability levels.

Take Away Reading speed is important. The Common Core includes improving reading speed as one of the key means to improve student outcomes (NGA & CCSSO, 2010a). Tests are timed, and ELLs, whose reading speeds are lower than their NES peers, are at a disadvantage on any test (even math, science, or history) when their reading speed lags substantially behind. Also, reading is increasingly the medium of learning at the upper grade levels. ELLs who read slowly cannot keep up with the homework demands of their classes. A combination of sustained intensive and extensive reading activities is necessary to help ELLs catch up to their NES peers.

Fluency

Consider the following questions:
- *What does it mean to read fluently?*
- *How is fluent reading related to reading comprehension?*
- *How can teachers prepare ELLs to read more fluently?*

Reading requires not only that students read quickly but that they comprehend the text. Reading comprehension requires that students maintain flow, with a sense of intonation and rhythm natural to the language, a sense of fluency (Grabe, 2004; Kuhn & Stahl, 2003; National Reading Panel, 2000). NES students have normally gained this ability through years of reading practice, though students with documented reading difficulties have not, and thus require focused reading fluency training (Taylor, 2011; Taylor & Spichtig, 2011).

ELLs without oral fluency in English are at a disadvantage (Kuhn & Stahl, 2003; Morrow, Kuhn, & Schwanenflugel, 2006). They may even be labeled as special needs students because of their low scores on reading assessments. When ELLs begin to read, they tend to focus on one word at a time, which prevents them from gaining a sense of how ideas are connected to each other. Imagine a computer reading program that puts equal stress on each word and never varies the speed. Even simple sentences become difficult to understand:

ifyouwanttounderstandacomplextextitisimportanttobefluent

So a focus on reading speed needs to be tempered with the need for fluency (Grabe, 2004, 2009). In-class intensive reading activities can improve students' overall reading ability over time. Fluency activities that emphasize eye movement and focus on specific words in a text can help (Bar-Kochva, 2013; Grabe & Stoller 2002; Taylor & Spichtig, 2011). Scanning activities that ask students to find specific words in a text, or to see how quickly they can count the number of nouns in a paragraph, provide practice moving and pausing a student's gaze as he or she addresses a text. Other methods that have been shown to improve reading fluency can easily be adapted to the content-area classroom. Modeling, repeated reading, extensive reading, and reading while listening are highly recommended for ELLs at all grade levels. These techniques have proven to be effective if the reading material is at an appropriate ability level (as opposed to the standard grade level) and culturally appropriate for the ELLs.

Combining the receptive skills of reading and listening is a common practice for children learning to read, but is seldom used in the upper grades. However, reading while listening can be a useful tool for building reading fluency (Popko, 2009), given that there are strong correlations between silent reading and reading fluency (Bar-Kochva, 2013).

Modeling

Consider the following questions:
- *How do students know which parts of a reading text are important to remember?*
- *How can teachers scaffold ELL learners' reading process, when most reading is done silently?*

When NES children are beginning to learn to read, parents and teachers often read aloud to them. Hearing the words as they follow along supports learning by reinforcing the sound/symbol correspondence. However, by middle school, students seldom hear a fluent adult reading from their textbooks. ELLs have often not had the same background while learning to read English. Teachers can scaffold ELLs' reading process by reading aloud in a couple of ways.

Teachers can help by modeling how English breaks down into meaningful chunks (Grabe, 2009; Echevarria, Vogt, & Short, 2004). Learning that phrases are natural pausing points, along with commas and periods, can help ELLs train their eyes to glide across text rather than stuttering across each word. A simple exercise to demonstrate the flow and rhythm of English would be to have students mark a line across the text whenever the teacher pauses.

First, teachers can use a think-aloud protocol while reading a difficult text. Starting with previewing the chapter, teachers can model suggested reading behaviors for ELLs. While reading the title, headings, and captions, the teacher can use techniques like questioning the text, prediction, and guessing at new vocabulary words. Using an overhead projector, the teacher can also highlight relevant information and take notes on the text.

The second modeling process is to ask students to read along silently as the teacher reads aloud. This technique is often used in lower levels, but disappears in higher grades, largely because most NES students can read silently faster than someone can read aloud (Manning, Lewis, & Lewis, 2010). However, reading while listening can benefit ELLs even at advanced levels. A less intrusive method is to get students to read a text while listening to a recorded copy (Popko, 2011). ELLs benefit from hearing the natural rhythm and flow of English. They learn how to pronounce English words in context, and how to spell words that they only knew orally. The teacher may wish to pause occasionally to remark on particular ideas that are central to the content, or to make connections to prior readings.

These modeling strategies are important for teachers in every academic field. It is important for students to understand how math, science, or history texts should be approached. For ELLs, it is also useful to choose culturally situated texts that represent the ELLs' home cultures. Reading such culturally appropriate texts can be highly engaging, and demonstrates the teachers' respect for and appreciation of the ELLs' home cultures. Such texts can be easily integrated into strategy instruction in English language arts (ELA) and history classes, but even in math or science classes the teacher might choose a biography or article about someone in an ELL student's country to illustrate a key point.

New technologies on tablets, such as Kindle's *Whispersync* software, and apps such as those produced by *Grasshopper Apps* allow students to read, listen, or do both at the same time. At this point, the books available in this format tend to be novels and popular trade books, so schools may need to record their own versions of the textbooks that are to be used by ELLs.

Note that this does not include having students read aloud. When ELLs are called upon to vocalize English, they often get nervous, and they tend to focus on decoding the text and on proper pronunciation, which lowers their comprehension of the whole text.

Take Away ELLs benefit from having a fluent NES model reading aloud. Teachers can use oral modeling of reading to help ELLs understand difficult texts. Reading while listening to audiobooks can also help.

Repeated Reading

Consider the following questions:
- *How many times do young children read the same picture book?*
- *How many times do good readers read their favorite novels?*
- *What would be the benefit of reading the same text more than once?*

One method that has been used with NES children at beginning levels of reading is repeated reading (Samuels, 1979). The basic idea is to allow children to read and reread high-interest books to improve fluency and automaticity (Samuels, 2004). The first reading will tend to be slow, with students stopping many times to check comprehension. Speed will improve with repeated readings, until a given reading begins to become boring. Then a new reading is chosen and the process repeats.

Repeated reading uses interesting stories from graded readers that are read repeatedly with students keeping track of their own reading speeds (in wpm). The target speed is 250 wpm at 12th grade (Taylor & Spichtig, 2011), or 2 minutes for each 500-word reading. Like reading while listening, repeated reading has been used more often at lower levels of reading ability. However, Gorsuch's and Taguchi's (2008) longitudinal analysis of this system, in which "learners read specified passages from graded readers (books that have reduced vocabulary range and simplified grammatical structures) repeatedly in order to increase learners' sight recognition of words and to develop automaticity in lower-level processing (p. 28)" demonstrates that repeated reading can benefit ELLs at higher reading proficiency levels as well.

Take Away Often ELLs are not provided with opportunities to learn to read in the same way that NES children do. Reading typically assigned in content course textbooks tends to be low interest and high pressure because comprehension will be tested. It is also typically the case that ELLs, because of their slower reading speeds, will only read an assigned chapter once.

Extensive Reading to Increase Comprehension

Consider the following questions:
- How much do students read?
- How is the amount of reading related to reading comprehension?
- How can content teachers encourage ELLs to read extensively?

In their 13-year-long longitudinal study of the reading habits of a cohort of K–12 students in Canada, Cunningham and Stanovich (1997) found that students who engaged in extensive pleasure reading outside of the classroom enjoyed gains in test scores in every subject over their peers who did not read extensively. The students who read fewer than 50,000 words (about one novel) per year outside of class fell in the lowest 5% of test scores for the group across the board. Those who were in the top 5% averaged 5 million words (about 100 novels) per year outside of class. There were strong correlations between number of words read and test scores for the whole group.

The reason for these differences is related to the well-documented reading spiral (Stanovich, 1986, and elsewhere): (a) If a student doesn't read well, the student doesn't like to read. (b) A student who doesn't like to read doesn't read as much as a student who does. (c) Reading less causes the student not to read well. The cycle repeats. On the other hand, (a) a student who reads well likes to read. (b) When a student likes to read, the student reads more. (c) When a student reads more, the student reads better. Thus the upward spiral continues.

Several suggestions have been made to change the direction of the downward spiral. Interventions at each of the three stages have been proposed. Many extensive reading programs focus on improving motivation in order to help students enjoy reading (thus reading more, thus reading better). Keys to encouraging extensive reading in the classroom include

1. Provide students access to a wide variety of books, and let them choose what to read. Books should be at a variety of difficulty levels based on the average ability of the class, from two levels lower than a students' average ability level to two levels over the target for the class, and should cover different genres. The books should be culturally appropriate for a specific group of students.

2. Provide a comfortable space where students can read.

3. Establish regular periods of sustained silent reading (Manning, Lewis, & Lewis, 2010) when all students are expected to read their chosen books.

4. Monitor the students' reading, but don't judge. Students should chart what and how much they are reading, and be able to discuss it, but tests on content are not advised.

5. Get students to share with their peers—reviewing, rating, or recommending good books to each other. This might be a daily oral book report on what students are reading, posting of reviews on the word wall, or just a chart listing the students' names, the titles of their current books, and their stars earned. One of the most common methods is for students to keep a journal that they write in every day listing the reading title, author, amount of time spent reading, number of pages read, a one- to two-sentence summary of the day's reading, a prediction of what will happen next, or any other method of briefly interacting with the text.

6. Model the process—all of the teachers and administrators in the school should participate in the reading and sharing, with their own charts or reports posted in a public place in the school.

7. Some sort of benchmark recognition should be established (1 book = 1 silver star, 10 silver stars = 1 gold star).

8. Allow students to bring in their own books, and to take books home with them.

9. When ELLs are literate in their own language but cannot yet read in English, allow them to participate by reading in their home language.

Take Away Extensive reading, which has been demonstrated to improve student performance in NES populations, will also benefit ELLs. However, unlike NES students, ELLs come to the activity with lower vocabulary, developing grammar, lower reading speeds, less fluency, and a wider range of reading abilities. Therefore it is important to scaffold ELL extensive reading by providing a wider difficulty range of reading materials, posting publicly visible benchmarks, and having teachers and administrators model the program.

Reading While Listening

Consider the following questions:
- *How do children learn to read in their own language?*
- *How are oral language and literacy related?*
- *How can educators use reading while listening activities to improve students' reading skills?*

The majority of children in any culture learn oral language first.[5] It would be silly to imagine a baby who cannot yet speak being taught to read. Yet in the United States, every year, ELLs who cannot speak English are being asked to read and write, and their school grades are dependent on their reading ability. Although there are some differences between first- and second-language acquisition, the reality is that language is oral in nature and the spoken form of the language is a necessary stage in learning to read.

As stated earlier, NES students enter school with around 5,000 words of vocabulary, but possibly no ability to read. ELLs need to work on their oral vocabulary before being taught to read. Over time, NES students develop a literate vocabulary that is much wider than their oral vocabulary, because authors use many words that are not a part of daily conversation. In fact, authors frequently expand their own vocabularies while writing by referring to dictionaries, textbooks, and cited written sources when writing and editing their work. ELLs are playing vocabulary catch-up throughout their school years, and so need more oral support than NES students for a longer period of time.

Earlier, reading while listening was mentioned as a method of improving sound/symbol correspondence and increasing fluency. It can also support ELLs' reading comprehension at higher levels. Requiring the students to follow along in the book while listening to the audiobook provides a kind of scaffolding that

---

[5] Or, in the case of children who are hearing or speaking impaired, sign language. It is beyond the scope of this book to discuss sign language, but suffice it to say that it is a form of language based on the local superordinate language, that is, American Sign Language (ASL) is based on English structure, whereas Mexican Sign Language is based on Spanish structure.

may be missing from many sustained silent reading activities (Reutzel, Jones, & Newman, 2010). Words that NES students know orally but ELLs do not will often appear in textbooks, especially at the lower grade levels. Moreover, to the extent that pattern recognition supports reading comprehension (e.g., noticing that *comprehension* and *comprehend* have the same root and thus a similar meaning, or recognizing that the past participle is sometimes formed by adding –ed and sometimes by adding –en), NES students are ahead of their ELL peers. Reading while listening can help ELLs recognize patterns in the language that are oral in nature (e.g., alliteration, rhyme, syllable stress). However, the benefit of reading while listening depends on repetition of patterns. Therefore it needs to be an extensive rather than intensive activity.

At the lowest levels, ELLs can benefit from "read to me" books, which have become widely available as apps for hand-held devices. For intermediate levels, Voice of America has an app that shows transcripts of radio programs while the student is listening to the reports. At higher levels, Amazon has created software for the Kindle HD called *Whispersync*—many classic novels are already available for free on this platform—that allows students to read the book, listen to the audiobook, or do both at the same time. Once students learn this system of studying, schools might want to request audio versions of their textbooks, or even record them in house.

Reading while listening is a method that provides diminishing returns. Once a student gets to the point where she or he can read silently faster than the audiobook reads aloud, the task will become boring, and detrimental. ELLs can be asked to begin to read extensively at the level where this change occurs. However, once the difficulty of the text is increased, it is beneficial to allow the student to read while listening at that increased level of difficulty.

Teachers can use the technique in the classroom with all students by projecting a text on an overhead projector (from a physical book, computer screen, or tablet) while playing the audio. ELLs can also be allowed to use the reading while listening technique for their extensive reading activity (see pages 50 and 55).If the chosen book is something for light reading (like the VOA app), students might be asked to complete a reading more than once and react to it in a journal (perhaps even a vocabulary journal) or a report. Groups of ELLs can be asked to read the same text and discuss it in groups, or to read different texts and report on them to the rest of the group. Reading while listening texts at many different levels should be part of the class library, and any tablets used in class should have print/audio texts loaded on them for use during sustained silent reading (ELLs can use headphones).

Take Away Reading while listening is typically used in elementary school and discarded afterward, but it has gained increased attention as a useful method of increasing ELL reading abilities at all levels (including university English for academic purposes courses). It allows students to comprehend texts at a level higher than their demonstrated silent reading ability while training reading fluency, increasing reading speed, and building receptive vocabulary knowledge.

Practicing Strategies

Consider the following questions:
- *What strategies do you use when reading texts to learn new information?*
- *What is the role of reading strategy instruction in the K–12 setting?*
- *Can ELLs be expected to know how to use the same reading strategies used by successful NES students?*
- *How can teachers incorporate the teaching of reading strategies into the content-area classroom?*

When learning a language, it is important to teach more than the target vocabulary and grammar. ELLs not only need to learn English in class: They need to learn *how to learn* English in an ongoing manner. As with the difference between giving a man a fish and teaching a man to fish, getting students to understand today's lesson is not as useful as teaching them how to understand future lessons. In other words, simply giving students the meaning of language today (e.g., by translating) is not as useful for ELLs as teaching them language learning strategies that they can continue to apply in the future (Gersten et al., 2007).

Many of the language learning strategies that have been proposed in ESL literature are intended for use primarily in ESL classes. That is, classes in which all of the students are ELLs of approximately the same age and ability level. When considering strategies for teaching reading to ELLs in K–12, the focus should be on strategies that will help them (a) understand the required reading, (b) improve their reading ability (including speed, fluency, and comprehension), (c) improve their knowledge of English grammar, and d) increase their receptive and productive vocabulary (Freeman & Freeman, 2009).

All students, including ELLs, have preferred learning styles. Some benefit more from visual input, others from oral input. Some prefer deductive reasoning and others prefer inductive reasoning. To address these differences, teachers should present students with a wide range of reading strategies, focusing on, modeling, and practicing one at a time, and then allow students to choose which they will adapt in their own study process. An ESL student who chooses a handful of preferred strategies and uses them consistently will be more likely to improve than either the student who does not apply reading strategies or the student who changes strategies too often.

> **Take Away** ELLs should be taught to engage the text before, during, and after they read. From a teaching perspective, this requires that ELLs be taught prereading, during-reading, and postreading strategies (Grabe, 2009; Manchón, 2008; Sousa, 2011).

Prereading

Consider the following questions:
- *Before you read difficult material, what do you do to prepare?*
- *Can teachers predict what grammar and vocabulary will be difficult for ELLs before they assign the reading?*
- *How can teachers scaffold ELL comprehension of textbooks before the students begin reading?*

Establishing Background Knowledge

As mentioned earlier, ELLs cannot be assumed to come to any particular reading with the same knowledge of language, culture, or content as their NES peers. Therefore, activities that provide background knowledge should be provided for the student before beginning to read. These activities can be done in class with the whole class or in small groups, or they can be assigned as homework. Either way, the point is to situate the content of the reading within the curriculum, associate it with the students' prior knowledge, and establish the language (including difficult vocabulary and grammar) that will be required for the ELL to make sense of the text.

Warming Up

The teacher can begin activities connected to topics related to the target reading, rather than addressing the target reading directly. For example, if there is a reading on single-cell organisms in the text, the teacher might begin with a discussion of health: "What do we do before we leave the restroom to return to class? *Wash our hands.*" "Why don't we eat food that smells spoiled? *We might get sick.*" Lead the conversation to the idea of germs and bacteria, the concept that they are organisms that can be good or bad. A short discussion, pair work, or a list of questions provided in class with answers written at home and shared with the class can warm up the students to the topic of the day.

Another method of warming up students might be to play a game. In the case of single-cell organisms, you could play a game of sorting animals by size, then asking, "What is the smallest life form?" If the topic is to be the introductory chapter on the Civil War, you might play a game of "What happened on this date in _____?", going back by decades. In a math class introducing multiplication, you could ask "Isn't there an easier way?" starting by counting 100 beans, then having 10 students each count 10 beans and adding them together. Quick little activities that focus students' attention on the topic of a given reading help prepare ELLs for the task ahead.

Connecting to Students' Prior Knowledge

Highlighting prior knowledge about topics related to a target reading can stimulate students' ability to focus on and comprehend the target texts. Activities that can help establish each student's prior knowledge and help the student connect that knowledge to the target reading are particularly useful in diverse classrooms. With NES students, it is often enough to ask the class "What do you know about _____?" However, a bit more effort is needed to establish what a group of ELLs' prior knowledge on a subject is, and to then connect that prior knowledge to the topic of the target reading. Rather than put a general question to a group of students, it is important to gather individual feedback from each ELL. What the exchange student from Germany knows might differ widely from what the child whose parents recently emigrated from Sudan knows about any given topic.

One method that can be used (if the ELLs are able to write sufficiently) is a brief written pretest. For example, the teacher could ask students to define key vocabulary related to the topic (five or six words). The teacher might ask students to write down words or phrases that they associate with the topic of the target reading, perhaps prompting their memory by showing photographs that portray related subjects (e.g., if the topic is single-cell organisms, the teacher can show magnified slides of a leaf collected in a prior lesson that shows the cells). Students can then write about what they see and what they remember about that lesson.

When ELLs are not sufficiently capable of writing, a method for connecting to prior knowledge is to have students organize pictures. For example, prior to reading about the Civil War, the students could place pictures of people in period dress on a timeline. Before studying the food chain, students could place pictures of animals into groups (e.g., dividing mammals from reptiles, or vertebrates from invertebrates). Students might also be asked to place sentences or pictures in order, demonstrating a process that they need to know prior to reading the target text (e.g., filling in a diagram of the water cycle before discussing water pollution).

A third method of entering a new text that is culturally situated within the U.S. educational setting would be to provide a short prereading about the ELLs' home cultures. Teachers can find such readings that correspond to difficult passages in a given textbook or write short passages themselves, if the school in question has a relatively stable population of ELLs with the same background.

If students come from a variety of cultures, the teacher can ask older students to write short passages that can be filed and used with younger students.

> **Take Away** Teachers realize that no student is a *tabula rasa* arriving in class. Getting students to connect the knowledge they bring with them to class to the content of the texts they have to read provides ELLs with a strategy that many native speakers of a language bring to any text that they read. Time spent teaching and modeling techniques for accessing prior knowledge can improve ELL reading speed, fluency, and comprehension of texts. Explicitly connecting new course material to students' background knowledge also provides ELLs with a useful strategy that they can apply to any new reading they encounter.

Situating the Reading in Context

Consider the following questions:
- *Where do the courses you teach fit into your school's curriculum?*
- *Are readings in your school chosen to prepare students for statewide exams?*
- *Do the readings you choose stem from prior readings?*
- *Do you use reading assignments to build knowledge students need for readings in future classes?*

K–12 curricula are increasingly based on external standards such as the Common Core (NGA & CCSSO, 2010a). One benefit of such standards-based curricula is that lessons are not isolated or disconnected. Rather, they are placed in a systematic way that should build from week to week, semester to semester, year to year. For ELLs this systematic approach provides continuity of effort. It is important that rather than approaching each reading task as a new activity that presents only new information, teachers should situate each reading in the context of the unit, the class, and the curriculum. What readings led up to this point? How will this reading contribute to the understanding of future course materials? What vocabulary is needed to comprehend this reading, and what vocabulary will be learned from it and applied to future texts?

Until recently, educational leaders have assumed that students who learn an idea or process in one class can transfer that knowledge to a different class. For example, it has been assumed that students who learn to read in ELA or ESL classes will transfer that skill and be able to apply it to reading in math and science classes. Recent research indicates that this is not necessarily the case (August & Shanahan, 2006; NGA & CCSSO, 2010a; Cummins, 2000; Freeman & Freeman, 2009; Genesee et al., 2006; Grabe, 2009). Especially with ELLs, if teachers want the students to apply what they learn in one class setting to another, the teacher must help the student by providing explicit connections. Vocabulary learned in the science classroom will not necessarily be remembered in English class. Writing conventions taught in ELA and ESL classes are not automatically used when writing for history class. In fact, students do not systematically apply what they have learned in one semester to the material they are studying in the following semester.

Prior to reading a new chapter or article it is therefore useful for teachers to prepare ELLs by making explicit connections to prior learning. One system for situating new readings in context is to create annual, monthly, and daily class objectives, and to post them on the board. Recently, these have been organized as "Can do" statements (World-Class Instructional Design and Assessment, 2008). ELLs benefit most from objectives when: (a) the presentation of objectives is systematic and consistent, and (b) there are English language objectives as well as content objectives. To build objectives into a system, the teacher should

1. Create a list of daily objectives based on both content and language standards before the semester begins.

2. Write the daily objectives on the board (or use an overhead) before class begins.

3. Begin class by sharing the objectives with students.

4. Return to the daily objectives throughout the lesson as each one is covered.

5. Assess whether or not the daily objectives have been met at the end of each class.

6. Regularly assess and revise future objectives if the daily objectives are being met more quickly than anticipated, or if they are not being met.

Take Away In order to help ELLs master the English language, not just comprehend the content (they will, eventually, be required to demonstrate their comprehension of content using adequate English writing) the teacher should include language skills and knowledge within the course and daily objectives.

During-Reading

Consider the following questions:
- *What do you do as you are reading a difficult new text that you need to study?*
- *What is the difference between the strategies used by good readers and those used by less capable readers?*
- *What strategies can teachers use to scaffold ELLs' comprehension and memory of texts while the students are reading?*

The act of reading is most commonly and efficiently done as an individual activity. NES students perform best on reading tasks when reading silently. ELLs also need to learn how to read silently, but if a text is above their ability level, they can benefit from listening to the text as they read along. Either way, reading is essentially an individual task. In order to encourage ELLs to focus their attention on the important aspects of the reading, it can be useful to assign a task for them to accomplish as they read.

The complexity of a during-reading task will vary depending on the length of the reading, the gap between the students' reading abilities and the difficulty of the text, and the purpose of the task. When teaching students how to understand new vocabulary in context, a short, relatively easy text with 5–10 unknown words can be used. In that case, the during-reading task may be more time consuming and complex because the purpose of the reading is not general comprehension of the content.

However, keep in mind that reading comprehension can be compromised if the during-reading task is too intrusive. Simple, quick tasks that don't disturb the general flow of the reading work best. These tasks should bring students' attention to key points in the text without slowing down the students reading rate. During-reading activities that work well are tasks such as underlining or highlighting, numbering, and other forms of taking notes in the text. Activities that should be discouraged include looking up words in a dictionary, writing long answers to a set of questions, outlining the text, and writing a summary. Such time-consuming tasks ought to be performed as pre- or postreading activities. Instructions for during-reading tasks might include:

- Highlight the names of the children in the story.

- Number each step in the process in the margins of the text.

- Put a star in the margin by each new invention the author mentions.

- Underline any new words you find in the story.

- Underline any passive voice sentences you see.

- Highlight information you think may be on the test.

When ELLs first learn to highlight text as they read, they have a tendency to highlight everything because "it is all important." Teachers should model the marking of a text to help students recognize how to perform the task. They may need to model each new during-reading task they assign, so that ELLs who may not understand the oral instructions can learn by example.

During-reading activities should not be used for extensive reading activities. Extensive reading should be enjoyable and interesting for the student, so the text used should be based on the actual reading level of the student, not on grade level or target level. Any task that takes the student's focus away from basic comprehension of the text or that reduces student enjoyment of the book should be avoided.

Take Away ELLs can benefit from two types of during-reading tasks: complex tasks focused on learning language that are performed on short, easily read texts, and simple tasks for study reading that focus the students' attention on key information or text structure in longer readings (like textbook chapters). When the focus is on extensive reading, the only task should be to read and comprehend a long text, such as a book.

Postreading

Consider the following questions:
- *Once you have read a difficult text that contains information you would like to apply, what do you do to ensure you remember the key information?*
- *What do you do to encourage your students to work with a text, after they have read it, to ensure comprehension and memory of the key points?*
- *What postreading strategies can teachers assign in order to scaffold ELLs' ability to comprehend and remember the key points of the reading?*

Postreading activities are probably the most commonly used in classes. Typically, teachers ask NES students to answer comprehension questions, discuss the reading as a whole class, or summarize the reading. Course readings are also the primary source of items on quizzes and unit tests. There is often the assumption that the reading is appropriate for the level. Therefore, students should be able to complete these tasks if they have done the reading.

It should not be assumed that ELLs who have done the reading can complete these types of assessment tasks. Prior to testing ELLs' knowledge of the reading, it is useful to ask them to perform some postreading learning activities. There is a difference between NES student and ELL vocabulary levels and grammar. Postreading activities that focus on language are an important means of bridging this gap. Moreover, ELLs must focus more of their cognitive attention on the language itself. Therefore, less of an ELL's cognitive attention may be focused on content and memory.

Therefore, postreading activities for ELLs should focus on learning English, understanding the content better, and remembering the key points. Well-crafted postreading tasks take ELLs back to the text and prepare them for the quizzes and tests to come. While during-reading tasks should be largely silent and solo, postreading tasks can be beneficial when performed as pair or group activities. ELLs can learn from other ELLs or from their NES peers, not just from the teacher and the textbook.

Language focused postreading tasks should place a strong emphasis on learning how to create meaning from the text. The emphasis can be on grammar, vocabulary, or textual organization and cohesion. Grammar tasks might include:

- Mark all of the subjects in the text and draw arrows connecting them to their verbs (perhaps followed by writing a list of each S/V combination).

- Mark the pronouns and draw arrows to the nouns to which they refer.

- Put parentheses around all the prepositional phrases.

- Make a list of adjectives in the text.

- Rewrite complex sentences in the text as simple sentences.

- Underline the topic sentences.

Unlike NES students, ELLs need to expand their vocabulary by learning new Tier 1 and Tier 2 words. They also need to learn different meanings for words they already know (e.g., some of the 20 definitions for *head*), different forms of words (e.g., define → definition), and synonyms. When assigning postreading tasks for vocabulary, teachers should remember not to focus only on the target content vocabulary of the lesson (which is typically Tier 3 vocabulary from fourth grade and up). Some of the words targeted by the task should be those that ELLs don't know and that appear often in the subject matter. For example, in the example from the science text (page 44), *twirl* and *rotate* might be known to most NES fifth-graders, but they will be difficult for ELLs. Also, ELLs should be asked to perform tasks that will provide them with useful vocabulary learning strategies, like using an appropriate dictionary. Postreading vocabulary instructions might include:

- Highlight 10 words you don't know and look them up in a learner's dictionary.

- Highlight words that will be on the exam, from the list provided.

- List words from the text that rhyme with *function*.

- Highlight the negative words in the text (e.g., those beginning with im–, in–, il–, un–, non–), and make a list of their positive equivalents.

- Find synonyms in the text for words from the list provided.

- Use the words from any of the previous tasks to write sentences about the content of the reading.

Authors utilize textual cohesion devices in order to help the reader follow the logic of the text. The purpose is to be to make the reading easier. However, ELLs might find such devices confusing, making it harder for them to comprehend the text. Postreading tasks that help ELLs see the structure of the text and how the author uses language to achieve cohesion will improve reading ability. Some tasks that can accomplish this include:

- Highlight the transition words (e.g., first, then, moreover) in the text.

- Write a one-sentence summary of each paragraph, and then combine those sentences into a one-paragraph summary of the text. (Such summaries can be saved and used as age-, ability-, and culture-appropriate prereading activities in future classes.)

- Circle the main topic of the text and draw lines connecting that topic to each word in the text that refers to that topic.

- Outline the text using sentences for level 1 (I, II, III), phrases for level 2 (A, B, C) and one or two words for level 3 (1, 2, 3).

- Draw a graphic organizer that represents the content, using key transition words from the text (e.g., a cycle, Venn diagram, process, or flow chart).

Postreading activities are occasionally overlooked in the rush of completing crowded curricula. NES students who are reading at grade level can be expected to read the material and study on their own to prepare for the test. However, ELLs often need guidance from the teacher in order to fully comprehend the language and content of required class readings.

Take Away Unlike NES students, ELLs are often not ready to learn content material from reading. Because they are not reading at the same level as NES students, ELLs need to be explicitly taught how to read and comprehend texts that are at their grade level. To scaffold ELL reading, it is a good idea to encourage them to engage with the same text multiple times, through a consistent process of assigning pre-, during-, and postreading activities.

Conclusion

6

Reading is a learned skill. NES children often learn the basic skills from parents, and arrive at school able to read. Even those NES students who are not reading by the time they enter school are typically prepared to read because they already know the English language. In school, their task is to decode the artifact that is writing in order to recognize that the symbols on the page represent language that they already know. They can then learn to reproduce those symbols as they learn to write.

English language learners (ELLs) do not have this common underlying knowledge. They often arrive in U.S. schools unable to speak and understand spoken English. Therefore, they cannot begin with the alphabet, with decoding the symbols. They must begin by building their oral knowledge of the language. Only when they have the basic vocabulary and a general understanding of English grammar can they begin to learn how to read.

Reading is not natural. It takes effort: Training, study, and practice. According to the International Reading Association, "all language learners—whether they are infants just beginning to speak, older children learning to read and write, or adults acquiring a second language or a new professional vocabulary— learn language by using it purposefully and negotiating with others" (NCTE, 2012b, p. 14). Even though NES students come to school reading or ready to learn to read, it takes years (typically first through third grade) to teach them how to read well enough to be able to learn new information from textbooks (typically at fourth grade). Literacy is an ongoing quest. NES students struggle (and often fail) to keep up with the increasing literacy demands of school throughout their education. A student might continue only through high school, go on to college or university, take a master's degree, or even pursue a doctoral degree: The bar is raised at each level. To continue education is to continue adding breadth and depth of vocabulary knowledge and sentence structure.

It is a common mistake to assume that ELLs know how to read because of their age or grade level. Unfortunately, many ELLs do not read in their own languages, let alone in English. In order for them to keep up with target learning goals, ELLs need to receive reading instruction at every grade level in every subject. They also need adapted material at their reading level that meets the subject area standards.

U.S. NES students have recently been falling behind in reading. A primary reason for this is their limited vocabulary. The Common Core Standards (NGA & CCSSO, 2010b) place a strong emphasis on teaching vocabulary across the curriculum as key to overcoming this problem. Even though this decrease in student vocabulary knowledge has been well documented, NES students still have a huge advantage over ELLs in words known at each grade level.

Depending on the age at which they entered U.S. schools, ELLs probably know a limited amount of vocabulary and grammar. However, they will not have caught up to the level of vocabulary known by their NES peers (see Figure 1). Given the recent focus on teaching vocabulary in every subject area and at all grade levels, it is clear that ELLs require more support in the form of direct vocabulary teaching.

NES students begin by learning to read personal narratives. They then read narrative fiction of increasing lengths. They are transitioned into reading informational texts by fourth grade. Each year thereafter, the difficulty level of the informational texts they are expected to read increases.

ELLs come to the United States typically not having had this gradual introduction to genres. If they arrive in the upper grades, they may not have been taught to read narrative. At whatever grade they enter, they will certainly not have been taught to read English textbooks to get information. A 6-month intensive course, a 1-hour pullout class, or an unstructured immersion experience will not meet their needs. Sustained engagement in reading in every subject area is needed. This requires focused teaching that builds ELLs' sociocultural and educational background knowledge, develops their vocabulary at all three tiers, teaches them English structure, and provides them with ample opportunities for extensive practice.

References and Further Reading

References

August, D., & Shanahan, T. (Eds.). (2006). *Developing literacy in second-language learners: A report of the National Literacy Panel on language minority children and youth.* Mahwah, NJ: Lawrence Erlbaum Associates.

Bar-Kochva, I. (2013). What are the underlying skills of silent reading acquisition? A developmental study from kindergarten to the 2nd grade. *Reading and Writing: An Interdisciplinary Journal, 26,* 1417–1436.

Barone, D. M., & Xu, S. H. (2008). *Literacy instruction for English language learners PreK–2.* New York, NY: Guilford Press.

Beck, I. L., & McKeown, M. G. (1985). Teaching vocabulary: Making the instruction fit the goal. *Educational Perspectives, 23*(1), 11–15.

Beck, I. L., McKeown, M. G., & Omanson, R. C. (1987). *The effects and uses of diverse vocabulary instructional techniques.* In M. G. McKeown & M. E. Curtis (Eds.), *The nature of vocabulary acquisition* (pp. 147–163). Hillsdale, NJ: Erlbaum.

Breznitz, Z. (2006). *Fluency in reading: Synchronization of processes.* Mahwah, NJ: Lawrence Erlbaum Associates.

Carroll, L. (1875). *Through the looking glass.* The Millennium Fulcrum Edition 1.7. Retrieved from http://www.gutenberg.org/files/12/12-h/12-h.htm

Carver, R. P. (1994). Percentage of unknown vocabulary words in text as a function of the relative difficulty of the text: Implications for instruction. *Journal of Reading Behavior, 26*(4), 413–437.

Council of Europe. (2011). *Common European framework of reference for languages: Learning, teaching, assessment.* Strasbourg, France: Author.

Coxhead, A. (2000). A new academic word list. *TESOL Quarterly, 34,* 213–238.

Cummins, J. (1979). Cognitive/academic language proficiency, linguistic interdependence, the optimum age question and some other matters. *Working Papers on Bilingualism, 19,* 121–129.

Cummins, J. (2000). *Language, power, and pedagogy: Bilingual children in the crossfire.* Clevedon, England: Multilingual Matters.

Cummins, J. (2005). Teaching the language of academic success: A framework for school-based language policies. In C. F. Leyba (Ed.), *Schooling and language minority students: A theoretical framework* (3rd ed., pp. 3–31). Los Angeles, CA: Evaluation, Dissemination and Assessment Center, California State University, Los Angeles.

Cunningham, A. E., & Stanovich, K. E. (1997). Early reading acquisition and its relation to reading experience and ability 10 years later. *Developmental Psychology 1997, 33,* 934–945.

Echevarria, J., Vogt, M. E., & Short, D. (2004). *Making content comprehensible for English language learners: The SIOP model* (2nd ed.). Boston, MA: Allyn & Bacon.

Fillmore, L. W., & Snow, C. E. (2000). *What teachers need to know about language.* Washington, DC: U.S. Department of Education, Office of Educational Research and Improvement, Educational Resources Information Center.

Freeman, Y. S., & Freeman, D. E. (2009). *Academic language for English language learners and struggling readers: How to help students succeed across the content areas.* Portsmouth, NH: Heinemann.

Gardner, D., & Davies, M. (2014). A new academic vocabulary list. *Applied Linguistics, 35,* 305–327.

Genesee, F., Lindholm-Leary, K., Saunders, W. M., & Christian, D. (2006). *Educating English language learners: A synthesis of research evidence.* New York, NY: Cambridge University Press.

Gersten, R., Baker, S. K., Shanahan, T., Linan-Thompson, S., Collins, P., & Scarcella, R. (2007). *Effective literacy and English language instruction for English learners in the elementary grades.* Washington, DC: National Center for Education Evaluation and Regional Assistance, Institute of Education Sciences, U.S. Department of Education. Retrieved from http://ies.ed.gov/ncee/wwc/pdf/practice_guides/20074011.pdf

Gorsuch, G., & Taguchi, E. (2008). Repeated reading for developing reading fluency and reading comprehension: The case of EFL learners in Vietnam. *System, 36,* 253–278.

Grabe, W. (2004). Research on teaching reading. *Annual Review of Applied Linguistics, 24,* 44–69.

Grabe, W. (2009). *Reading in a second language: Moving from theory to practice.* New York, NY: Cambridge University Press.

Grabe, W., & Stoller, F. (2002). *Teaching and researching reading.* London, UK: Longman.

Hinsdale, B. A. (1896). *Teaching the language-arts: Speech, reading, composition.* New York, NY: D. Appleton and Company.

Hirsch, E. D., Jr., Kett, J. F., & Trefil, J. S. (1988). *Cultural literacy: What every American needs to know.* New York, NY: Random House.

Kaufman, D. (2007). *What's different about teaching reading to students learning English? Study Guide.* Washington, DC: Center for Applied Linguistics.

Klingner, J. K., Almanza, E., de Onis, C., & Barletta, L. M. (2008). Misconceptions about the second language acquisition process. In J. K. Klingner, J. J. Hoover, & L. M. Baca (Eds.), *Why do English language learners struggle with reading* (pp. 17–35). Thousand Oaks, CA: Corwin.

Krashen, S. (1981). *Second language acquisition and second language learning.* Oxford, England: Pergamon.

Kuhn, M. R., & Stahl, S. A. (2003). Fluency: A review of developmental and remedial practices. *Journal of Educational Psychology, 95,* 3–21.

Larsen-Freeman, D. (2001). Teaching grammar. In M. Celce-Murcia (Ed.), *Teaching English as a second or foreign language* (3rd ed., pp. 251–266). Boston, MA: Heinle & Heinle.

Larsen-Freeman, D. (2003). *Teaching language: From grammar to grammaring.* Boston, MA: Thomson/Heinle.

Laufer, B. (1989). What percentage of text-lexis is essential for comprehension? In C. Lauren & M. Nordman (Eds.), *Special language: From humans to thinking machines* (pp. 316–323). Clevedon, England: Multilingual Matters.

Laufer, B., & Nation, P. (1995) Vocabulary size and use: Lexical richness in L2 written production. *Applied Linguistics, 16*(3), 307–322.

Lee, D. (2013). *Borrowing from biology—nature's nanotechnology.* Retrieved from http://www.eduplace.com/science/hmsc/5/a/cricket/ckt_5a11.shtml

Lind, M. (1998, August 16). The beige and the black. *New York Times.* Retrieved from http://www.nytimes.com/1998/08/16/magazine/the-beige-and-the-black.html

Longman. (2014). *Dictionary of contemporary English online.* Retrieved from http://www.ldoceonline.com/

Manchón, R. M. (2008). Taking strategies to the foreign language classroom: Where are we now in theory and research? *IRAL, 46,* 221–243.

Manning, M., Lewis, M., & Lewis, M. (2010). Sustained silent reading: An update of the research. In E. H. Hiebert & D. R. Reutzel (Eds.), *Revisiting silent reading: New directions for teachers and researchers.* Newark, DE: International Reading Association.

Michel, J.-B., Shen, Y. K., Aiden, A. P., Veres, A., Gray, M. K., Pickett, J. P., Hoiberg, D., Clancy, D., Norvig, P., Orwant, J., Pinker, S., Nowak, M. A., & Aiden, E. L. (2011). Quantitative analysis of culture using millions of digitized books. *Science, 331,* 176–182.

Morrow, L. M., Kuhn, M. R., & Schwanenflugel, P. J. (2006). The family fluency program. *The Reading Teacher, 60,* 322–333.

Nagy, W. E. (2005). Why vocabulary instruction needs to be long-term and comprehensive. In E. F. Hiebert & M. L. Kamil (Eds.), *Teaching and learning vocabulary: Bringing research to practice* (pp. 27–44). Mahwah, NJ: Lawrence Erlbaum Associates.

Nagy, W. E., & Scott, J. A. (2014). Vocabulary processes. In M. Kamil, P. Mosenthal, P. Pearson, & R. Barr (Eds.), *Handbook of reading research* (Vol. 3, pp. 269–284). Mahwah, NJ: Lawrence Erlbaum Associates.

Nation, I. S. P. (1990). *Teaching and learning vocabulary.* Boston, MA: Newbury House.

Nation, I. S. P. (1993). Vocabulary size, growth and use. In R. Schreuder & B. Weltens (Eds.), *The bilingual lexicon* (pp. 115–134). Philadelphia, PA: John Benjamins.

National Council of Teachers of English. (2012a). *NCTE/CAEP standards for initial preparation of teachers of secondary English language arts, grades 7–12.* Retrieved from www.ncte.org/library/NCTEFiles/Groups/CEE/NCATE/ApprovedStandards_111212.pdf

National Council of Teachers of English. (2012b). *NCTE/IRA standards for the English language arts.* Retrieved from http://www.ncte.org/standards

National Governors Association Center for Best Practices & The Council of Chief State School Officers. (2010a). *Common Core State Standards.* Washington, DC: Authors.

National Governors Association Center for Best Practices & The Council of Chief State School Officers. (2010b). *Common Core State Standards for English language arts & literacy in history/social studies, science, and technical subjects.* Washington, DC: Authors. Retrieved from http://www.corestandards.org/ELA-Literacy

National Governors Association Center for Best Practices & The Council of Chief State School Officers. (2010c). *Common Core State Standards for English language arts & literacy in history/social studies, science, and technical subjects. Appendix A.* Washington, DC: Authors. Retrieved from http://www.corestandards.org/assets/Appendix_A.pdf

National Governors Association Center for Best Practices & The Council of Chief State School Officers. (2010d). *Application for English learners.* Washington, DC: Authors. Retrieved from http://www.corestandards.org/assets/application-for-english -learners.pdf

National Reading Panel. (2000). Teaching children to read: An evidence based assessment of the scientific research literature on reading and its implications for reading instruction (National Institute of Health Pub. No. 00-4769). Washington, DC: U.S. Department of Health and Human Services.

Neufeld, S. & Billuroğlu, A. (2006). *The bare necessities in Lexis: A new perspective on vocabulary profiling.* Retrieved from http://lextutor.ca/vp/bnl/BNL_Rationale.doc

No Child Left Behind (NCLB) Act of 2001, Pub. L. No. 107–110, § 115, Stat. 1425 (2002).

Orosco, M. J., de Schonewise, E. A., de Onis, C., Klingner, J. K., & Hoover, J. J. (2008). Distinguishing between language acquisition and learning disabilities among English learners. In J. K. Klingner, J. J. Hoover, & L. Baca (Eds.), *Why do English language learners struggle with reading: Language acquisition or learning disabilities?* (pp. 5–16). Thousand Oaks, CA: Corwin Press.

Oxford. (2014). *Advanced learner's dictionary online.* Retrieved from https://oald8 .oxfordlearnersdictionaries.com/

Phythian-Sence, C., & Wagner, R. (2007). Vocabulary acquisition: A primer. In R. K. Wagner, A. E. Muse, & K. R. Tannenbaum (Eds.), *Vocabulary acquisition: Implications for reading comprehension* (pp. 1–14). New York: Guilford Press.

Pilgreen, J. L. (2010). *English learners and the secret language of school.* Portsmouth, NH: Heinemann.

Popko, A. J. (2009). Demystifying presentation grading through student-created scoring rubrics. In T. Stewart (Ed.), *Insights on teaching speaking in TESOL* (pp. 179–190). Alexandria, VA: TESOL International Association.

Popko, A. J. (2011). Reading while listening to build receptive fluency. In N. Ashcroft & A. Tran (Eds.), *Teaching listening: Voices from the field* (pp. 105–114). Alexandria, VA: TESOL International Association.

Popko, A. J. (2014). *Teaching the youngest EFL students.* Manuscript submitted for publication.

Pressley, M., Disney, L., & Anderson, K. (2007). Landmark vocabulary instructional research and the vocabulary instructional research that makes sense now. In R. K. Wagner, A. E. Muse, & K. R. Tannenbaum (Eds.), *Vocabulary acquisition: Implications for reading comprehension* (pp. 205–232). New York, NY: Guilford Press.

Preston, B. (2013, July 3). *Homer Simpson's perfect car comes to life at 24 hours of LeMons. New York Times.* Retrieved from http://wheels.blogs.nytimes.com/2013/07/03 /homer-simpsons-perfect-car-comes-to-life-at-24-hours-of-lemons/?_php=true& _type=blogs&_r=0

Reutzel, D. R., Jones, C. D., & Newman, T. H. (2010). Scaffolded silent reading: Improving the conditions of silent reading practice in classrooms. In E. H. Hiebert & D. R. Reutzel (Eds.), *Revisiting silent reading: New directions for teachers and researchers.* Newark, DE: International Reading Association.

Samuels, S. J. (1979). The method of repeated readings. *The Reading Teacher, 32,* 403–408.

Samuels, S. J. (2004). Toward a theory of automatic information processing in reading revisited. In R. B. Ruddell, M. R. Ruddell, & H. Singer (Eds.), *Theoretical models and processes of reading* (5th ed., pp. 1127–1148). Newark, DE: International Reading Association.

Schmitt, N. (2008). Instructed second language vocabulary learning. *Language Teaching Research, 12,* 329–363.

Schmitt, N., Jiang, X., & Grabe, W. (2011). The percentage of words known in a text and reading comprehension. *The Modern Language Journal, 95,* 26–43.

Schmitt, N., & Schmitt, D. (2013). A reassessment of frequency and vocabulary size in L2 vocabulary teaching. *Language Teaching, 46,* 1–20.

Snow, C. E., & Kim, Y.-S. (2007). Large problems spaces: The challenge of vocabulary learning for English language learners. In R. K. Wagner, A. E. Muse, & K. R. Tannenbaum (Eds.), *Vocabulary acquisition: Implications for reading comprehension* (pp. 123–139). New York, NY: Guilford Press.

Sousa, D. (2008). *How the brain influences behavior: Management strategies for every classroom.* Thousand Oaks, CA: Corwin.

Sousa, D. (2011). *How the ELL brain learns.* Thousand Oaks, CA: Corwin.

Spargo, E. (2001). *Timed reading plus: Book 1.* Columbus, OH: Jamestown/Glencoe/Macmillan.

Stahl, S. (1999). *Vocabulary development.* Cambridge, MA: Brookline.

Stanovich, K. E. (1986). Matthew Effects in reading: Some consequences of individual differences in the acquisition of literacy. *Reading Research Quarterly, 21,* 360–407.

Stanovich, K. E. (2000). *Progress in understanding reading: Scientific foundations and new frontiers.* New York, NY: Guilford Press.

Stanovich, K. E., & Cunningham, A. E. (1993). Where does knowledge come from? Specific associations between print exposure and information acquisition. *Journal of Educational Psychology, 85,* 211–229.

Stanovich, K. E., & West, R. F. (1989). Exposure to print and orthographic processing. *Reading Research Quarterly, 24,* 402–433.

Stanovich, K. E., West, R. F., & Harrison, M. R. (1995). Knowledge growth and maintenance across the life span: The role of print exposure. *Developmental Psychology, 31,* 811–826.

Summer Institute of Linguistics. (2003). LinguaLinks Library, Version 5.0. [Computer software]. Dallas, TX: SIL International.

Syrja, R. C. (2011). *How to reach and teach English language learners.* San Francisco, CA: Jossey-Bass.

Taylor, S. E. (2011). The dynamic activity of reading. In S. E. Taylor (Ed.), *Exploring silent reading fluency: Its nature and development* (pp. 3–37). Springfield, IL: Charles C. Thomas.

Taylor, S. E., & Spichtig, A. (2011). Today's technology to develop silent reading proficiency and fluency. In S. E. Taylor (Ed.), *Exploring silent reading fluency: Its nature and development* (pp. 143–177). Springfield, IL: Charles C. Thomas.

TESOL International Association. (1997). *ESL standards for preK–12 students.* Alexandria, VA: Author.

TESOL International Association. (2006). *PreK–12 English language proficiency standards.* Alexandria, VA: Author.

TESOL International Association. (2010). *TESOL P–12 ESL professional teaching standards.* Alexandria, VA: Author.

U.S. Department of Education. (2013, June). *The biennial report to Congress on the implementation of the Title III state formula grant program: School years 2008–10.* Retrieved from http://www.ncela.gwu.edu/files/uploads/3/Biennial_Report_0810.pdf

Vygotsky, L. S. (1978). *Mind in society: The development of higher psychological processes.* Cambridge, MA: Harvard University Press.

Watkins, R., & Corry, M. (2014). *E-learning companion: Student's guide to online success* (4th ed.). Independence, KY: Cengage Learning. Retrieved from http://www.wadsworthmedia.com/marketing/sample_chapters/9781133316312_ch01.pdf

World-Class Instructional Design and Assessment. (2008). *Grade level cluster can do descriptors: The results of survey research.* Retrieved from http://www.wida.us/standards/CAN_DOs/

Zehr, M. A. (2010, October 1). Boston school system settles English language learners dispute with federal government. *Education Week.*

Additional Reading

August, D., & Shanahan, T. (Eds.). (2007). *Developing reading and writing in second-language learners: Lessons from the report of the NLP on language-minority children and youth.* New York, NY: Routledge.

Beck, I. L. (2006). *Making sense of phonics: The how's and why's.* New York, NY: Guilford Press.

Bourdieu, P. (1973). Cultural reproduction and social reproduction. In R. Brown (Ed.), *Knowledge, education, and cultural change: Papers in the sociology of education* (pp. 71–112). London, England: Tavistock.

Capps, R., Fix, M., Murray, J., Ost, J., Passel, J., & Herwanton, S. (2005). *The new demography of America's schools: Immigration and the No Child Left Behind Act.* Washington, DC: The Urban Institute.

Cummins, J. (1992). Language proficiency, bilingualism, and academic achievement. In P. Richard-Amato & M. A. Snow (Eds.), *The multicultural classroom: Readings for content-area teachers* (pp. 16–26). New York, NY: Longman.

Freeman, Y. S., Freeman, D. E., & Mercuri, S. (2002). *Closing the achievement gap: How to reach limited-formal-schooling and long-term English learners.* Portsmouth, NH: Heinemann.

Hirsch, E. D., Jr. (2006). *The knowledge deficit: Closing the shocking gap for American children.* Boston, MA: Houghton Mifflin.

Lado, A. (2012). *Teaching beginner ELLS using picture books.* Thousand Oaks, CA: Corwin.

Lonigan, C. J. (2007). Vocabulary development and the development of phonological awareness skills in preschool children. In R. K. Wagner, A. E. Muse, & K. R. Tannenbaum (Eds.), *Vocabulary acquisition: Implications for reading comprehension.* New York, NY: Guilford Press.

Popko, A. J. (2003). *Professionalization for graduate students in teaching English as a second language: Pathways and processes* (Unpublished doctoral dissertation, Northern Arizona University).

Popko, A. J. (2004). How MA-TESOL students use knowledge about language in teaching ESL classes. In N. Bartels (Ed.), *Applied linguistics and language teacher education* (pp. 387–404). New York, NY: Springer-Verlag.

Schmitt, N. (2010). *Researching vocabulary.* Basingstoke, England: Palgrave Macmillan.

Online Resources

3,000 Academic Words, Not Presented as Headwords
http://www.academicwords.info
http://www.alliance.brown.edu/
http://www.ascd.org/

**Application of Common Core State Standards
for English Language Learners**
http://www.corestandards.org/assets/application-for-english-learners.pdf

Boston Public Schools Settlement
http://legalclips.nsba.org/?p=2426

Center for Applied Linguistics
http://www.cal.org/

Common Core State Standards Initiative
http://www.corestandards.org/
http://www.corestandards.org/ELA-Literacy/
http://www.corestandards.org/Math/

Coxhead's Academic Word List
http://www.victoria.ac.nz/lals/resources/academicwordlist/

Dictionary of Contemporary English
http://www.ldoceonline.com/

The Global Language Monitor
http://www.languagemonitor.com/

Google/Harvard analysis
http://books.google.com/ngrams/

MacMillan Timed Reading Books
https://www.mheonline.com/program/view/4/22/2734/TIMEDREADS
/Title_Search

National Council of Teachers of English
http://www.ncte.org/

Oxford Advanced Learner's Dictionary
http://oald8.oxfordlearnersdictionaries.com/

Oxford 3000 Keywords
http://oald8.oxfordlearnersdictionaries.com/oxford3000/

Picture Dictionaries
http://visual.merriam-webster.com/
http://www.esolhelp.com/online-picture-dictionary.html
http://www.opdome.com/

Relevant Laws Pertaining to ELLs
http://www2.ed.gov/policy/landing.jhtml?src=pn

Research About Education
http://www.centeroninstruction.org/
http://ies.ed.gov/ncee/
http://nces.ed.gov/

Timed Reading Activity Online
http://college.cengage.com/collegesurvival/watkins/learning_companion/1e
/students/timed_reading.html

Vocabprofile
http://www.lextutor.ca/vp/bnl/

World Class Instructional Design and Assessment (WIDA) consortium
http://www.wida.us/
http://www.wida.us/standards/eld.aspx

Appendixes

Appendix A: *PreK–12 ESL Professional Teaching Standards* (TESOL, 2010)

Domain 1: Language

Candidates know, understand, and use the major concepts, theories, and research related to the nature and acquisition of language to construct learning environments that support ESOL students' language and literacy development and content area achievement.

Standard 1.a. Describing language. Candidates demonstrate understanding of language as a system and demonstrate a high level of competence in helping ESOL students acquire and use English in listening, speaking, reading, and writing for social and academic purposes.

Standard 1.b. Language acquisition and development. Candidates understand and apply concepts, theories, research, and practice to facilitate the acquisition of a primary and a new language in and out of classroom settings.

Domain 2: Culture

Candidates know, understand, and use the major concepts, principles, theories, and research related to the nature and role of culture and cultural groups to construct learning environments that support ESOL students' cultural identities, language and literacy development, and content-area achievement.

Standard 2.a. Nature and Role of Culture. Candidates know, understand, and use the major concepts, principles, theories, and research related to the nature and role of culture in language development and academic achievement that support individual students' learning.

Standard 2.b. Cultural Groups and Identity. Candidates know, understand, and use knowledge of how cultural groups and students' cultural identities affect language learning and school achievement.

Domain 3: Planning, Implementing, and Managing Instruction

Candidates know, understand, and use standards-based practices and strategies related to planning, implementing, and managing ESL and content instruction, including classroom organization, teaching strategies for developing and integrating language skills, and choosing and adapting classroom resources.

Standard 3.a. Planning for Standards-Based ESL and Content Instruction. Candidates know, understand, and apply concepts, research, and best practices to plan classroom instruction in a supportive learning environment for ESOL students. Candidates serve as effective English-language models, as they plan for multilevel classrooms with learners from diverse backgrounds using standards-based ESL and content curriculum.

Standard 3.b. Managing and Implementing Standards-Based ESL and Content Instruction. Candidates know, manage, and implement a variety of standards-based teaching strategies and techniques for developing and integrating English listening, speaking, reading, and writing, and for accessing the core curriculum. Candidates support ESOL students in accessing the core curriculum as they learn language and academic content together.

Standard 3.c. Using Resources Effectively in ESL and Content Instruction. Candidates are familiar with a wide range of standards-based materials, resources, and technologies, and choose, adapt, and use them in effective ESL and content teaching.

Domain 4: Assessment

Candidates understand issues of assessment and use standards-based assessment measures with ESOL students.

Standard 4.a. Issues of Assessment for ESL. Candidates understand various issues of assessment (e.g., cultural and linguistic bias; political, social, and psychological factors) in assessment, IQ, and special education testing (including gifted and talented); the importance of standards; and the difference between language proficiency and other types of assessment (e.g., standardized achievement tests of overall mastery), as they affect ESOL student learning.

Standard 4.b. Language Proficiency Assessment. Candidates know and use a variety of standards-based language proficiency instruments to inform their instruction and understand their uses for identification, placement, and demonstration of language growth of ESOL students.

Standard 4.c. Classroom-Based Assessment for ESL. Candidates know and use a variety of performance-based assessment tools and techniques to inform instruction.

Domain 5: Professionalism

Candidates demonstrate knowledge of the history of ESL teaching. Candidates keep current with new instructional techniques, research results, advances in the ESL field, and public policy issues. Candidates use such information to reflect upon and improve their instructional practices. Candidates provide support and advocate for ESOL students and their families and work collaboratively to improve the learning environment.

Standard 5.a. ESL Research and History. Candidates demonstrate knowledge of history, research, and current practice in the field of ESL teaching and apply this knowledge to improve teaching and learning.

Standard 5.b. Partnerships and Advocacy. Candidates serve as professional resources, advocate for ESOL students, and build partnerships with students' families.

Standard 5.c. Professional Development and Collaboration. Candidates collaborate with and are prepared to serve as a resource to all staff, including paraprofessionals, to improve learning for all ESOL students.

Appendix B: The SIOP Checklist

The Sheltered Instruction Observation Protocol (SIOP®)
(Echevarria, Vogt, & Short, 2000; 2004; 2008)

Observer(s): _____
Date: _____
Grade: _____
ESL Level: _____

Teacher: _____
School: _____
Class/Topic: _____
Lesson: Multi-day Single-day *(circle one)*

Total Points Possible: 120 (Subtract 4 points for each NA given) _____
Total Points Earned: _____   Percentage Score: _____

Directions: Circle the number that best reflects what you observe in a sheltered lesson. You may give a score from 0–4 (or NA on selected items). Cite under "Comments" specific examples of the behaviors observed.

	Highly Evident	Somewhat Evident		Not Evident	
Preparation	4	3	2	1	0
1. **Content objectives** clearly defined, displayed, and reviewed with students	❏	❏	❏	❏	❏
2. **Language objectives** clearly defined, displayed, and reviewed with students	❏	❏	❏	❏	❏
3. **Content concepts** appropriate for age and educational background level of students	❏	❏	❏	❏	❏
4. **Supplementary materials** used to a high degree, making the lesson clear and meaningful (e.g., computer programs, graphs, models, visuals)	❏	❏	❏	❏	❏
5. **Adaptation of content** (e.g., text, assignment) to all levels of student proficiency	❏	❏	❏	❏	❏
6. **Meaningful activities** that integrate lesson concepts (e.g., surveys, letter writing, simulations, constructing models) with language practice opportunities for reading, writing, listening, and/or speaking	❏	❏	❏	❏	❏

Comments:

	Highly Evident	Somewhat Evident		Not Evident	NA
Building Background	4	3	2	1	0	NA
7. **Concepts explicitly linked** to students' background experiences	❏	❏	❏	❏	❏	❏
8. **Links explicitly made** between past learning and new concepts	❏	❏	❏	❏	❏	
9. **Key vocabulary** emphasized (e.g., introduced, written, repeated, and highlighted for students to see)	❏	❏	❏	❏	❏	

Comments:

	Highly Evident	Somewhat Evident		Not Evident	
Comprehensible Input	4	3	2	1	0
10. **Speech** appropriate for students' proficiency level (e.g., slower rate, enunciation, and simple sentence structure for beginners)	❏	❏	❏	❏	❏
11. **Clear explanation** of academic tasks	❏	❏	❏	❏	❏
12. **A variety of techniques** used to make content concepts clear (e.g., modeling, visuals, hands-on activities, demonstrations, gestures, body language)	❏	❏	❏	❏	❏

Comments:

	Highly Evident	Somewhat Evident		Not Evident	
Strategies	4	3	2	1	0
13. Ample opportunities provided for students to use **learning strategies**	❏	❏	❏	❏	❏

(Reproduction of this material is restricted to use with Echevarria, Vogt, and Short [2008], *Making Content Comprehensible for English Learners: The SIOP® Model.*)

Echevarria, Jana J., Vogt, Maryellen, and Short, Deborah J. *Making Content Comprehensible For English Learners: The Siop Model* (3rd. ed.) ©2008. Printed and electronically reproduced by permission of Pearson Education, Inc., Upper Saddle River, New Jersey.

About the Author

Dr. Jeff Popko has taught ESOL in Japan, Hawaii, Spain, and Indonesia. He is a professor of ESL and TESOL at Eastern Michigan University, where he teaches and prepares teachers to teach English to speakers of other languages.